W9-BLH-224

FATHERHOOD
IS NOT PRETTY

GARY D. CHRISTENSON

ILLUSTRATED BY MIKE LESTER

Peachtree Publishers, Ltd.

Published by
PEACHTREE PUBLISHERS, LTD.
494 Armour Circle, N.E.
Atlanta, Georgia 30324

Text Copyright © 1986 Gary D. Christenson
Illustrations Copyright © 1986 Mike Lester

All rights reserved. No part of this book may be reproduced in any form
or by any means without the prior written permission of the Publisher,
excepting brief quotes used in connection with reviews, written specifically
for inclusion in a magazine or newspaper.

Manufactured in the United States of America

1st printing

Library of Congress Catalog Number 86-60008

ISBN 0-931948-91-6

For Debbie, Ben and Nate, my parents and all the special people in my life . . . and to my friend Jim, who would have laughed and understood.

Table of Contents

Preface:
From Here to Maternity

"A Father is a banker provided by nature."

French proverb

Fatherhood is not pretty. Give a listen to one who knows. It is loud. It is sticky. And it's mostly wet. It is demanding, unrelenting, onerous labor. Never forget that. Others will come to tell you differently. They will immerse you in the rhetoric of cute and proud. They are false prophets.

On the contrary, nature has given fathers a rather shabby position in the grand scheme of things. Like the prehistoric beast that crawls too soon from the slime only to find itself ill-suited to the environment, the father is immediately at odds with his new life. He is the dodo, the stegosaurus, the woolly mammoth of the human species. No special genetically-coded tricks for this poor slob. His cells care not for adaptation. He lumbers into his new role unaware of what 2 A.M. will bring, let alone tomorrow.

Consider: For nine months, nature goes to great lengths to ensure that a woman's body is ready for the task of parenting. It swells. It softens. It stores and builds. Like a split-level generating its own little family room, the woman's cells and hormones work three shifts to complete the exacting bodily modifications that childbirth requires. At gestation's end all systems will be tuned and ready to go, and the girl who used to ride on the back of your Suzuki will begin uttering profundities on such topics as nursing and bonding. She will suddenly be able to diaper a squalling infant like a rancher wrestling a calf to the brand. As though some floppy disk on child care had been inserted in her frontal lobe, she will handle with confidence and ease the job of motherhood.

But alas, the father, like a lemming plunging toward the sea, blindly pursues fatherhood, totally unprepared for the horrors that are to follow. Neither nature nor those who have gone before adequately acquaint him with the terrible events and miserable tasks in store.

No one, for instance, tells the father about the gruesome effects of dried rice cereal on shag carpeting, a compound so unyielding to soap and water, as well as power tools, that some have proposed its use in place of welds on automobile chassis. Nor does anyone describe for the expectant father the various contortions a child performs while having a diaper changed. (It's similar to Houdini trying to wrestle free from a straitjacket while dangling from a flagpole.)

In addition, the male who is soon to enter upon the bleak landscape of fatherhood is never told of the great loneliness he will endure in the company of those who do not share his zeal for this new undertaking. At no time will he be made more painfully aware of his social position than the first time he lets slip a fatherly anecdote during a business lunch.

Client: Waiter, I'll substitute cottage cheese for the baked potato, please.

Father: Cottage CHEESE . . . Boy oh boy! Last week we gave Little Ralph his first bowl of that stuff . . . Bound him up 'til Thursday, I mean to tell ya . . .

Similarly, no one bothers to warn the father that at least for the first year of fatherhood, the shoulders of every shirt he owns will bear the personal emblem of his child in the form of a spit-up stain. This is a lesser calamity, however, since spit-up stains can usually be camouflaged by a sport coat.

But, no doubt, the most horrific change for the father is having his available cash removed from him regularly as pediatricians, shoe stores, toy manufacturers, diaper services, photographers and other predators feast off his wallet like crows after roadkill. In no time at all, they will pick his carcass clean, leaving him to wander through life with an empty passbook and last year's Hush Puppies.

Not a very pretty sight, to say the least. However, there are ways for the father to cut his losses. First, he would be wise to keep his family small. (A Christmas Club account can best be spent on a vasectomy.) In addition, a job that requires long hours away from home and family will provide that necessary buffer between the father and those frequent urges to hurl himself off the top of the utility shed. And last, eighteen or twenty years is really not such a long time. Look at Papillon or the Birdman of Alcatraz; they made it. Of course, the latter may not be a wholly fair comparison. After the orthodontist has been paid, remember, there's not a lot of money left to spend on pigeons.

Yes, contemporary fatherhood is a good deal different from what it once was. I grew up in a traditional environment and little realized that my own father was the last of a breed.

"Get yer feet off the coffee table or I'm gonna kick yer butt up into yer head." Boy, they don't make fathers like that anymore. He never needed Phil Donahue to set him straight about anything. He had no qualms about blazing new parental territory all by himself. Long before anyone ever had heart-to-hearts with kids about sex, my old man was giving it to us straight. "Touch it and you'll go as crazy as yer Aunt Veronica after the change," he said. And as far as premarital sex was concerned, "Sure you can, long as you don't mind having a disease that covers you in festering sores."

But since his wise advice was first uttered, fathers in this country have lost something, and that's good old common fatherly sense: the kind of innate stuff that tells you how to set the spark on a '49 Hudson and the best time of day to fish for suckers and shiners. Nope, as my Uncle Buck would have put it, "a bunch of wise-ass media folk have gone and made a whole lot out of a little," meaning that he had about as much use for anyone who needed to be taught parenting as he did for "one of them sissy poodle dogs from the city."

The trouble is there are so many "authorities" raving about fatherhood these days that everyone is pretty confused about what to do, what to say, what to buy and where to get it. There must be a few hundred books out there telling everybody what a joyful experience the whole thing is. Of course, only a father who has suffered a blow to the frontal lobe with a blunt object would ever spout such nonsense. Anyone who has ever fathered for any amount of time will tell you that the whole thing is about as much fun as slipping off the seat of a boy's bicycle. But no one wants to write a book like that . . . well, almost no one.

Fatherhood Is Not Pretty tells it straight. Believe me, I've been there. For guys doomed by impending fatherhood, this book will let you know a little of what's in store. No cutesy psychological stuff. Just straight over-the-counter advice from one of your own. And you veterans . . . you'll see yourselves on these pages, too. That's why I wrote this thing, and that's the way Uncle Buck would want it.

Part I

The Expectant Father

L ike the lions of the jungle and the wildebeest of the plains, he is at once fearsome and fearful. He looks out upon a world he thought was his, but the world stares back mockingly. He is the expectant father, a hunted beast whose time as a predator of Italian loafers and imported beer draws short. For the world is closing in, reaching out to trap and imprison him with bonds of whole life premiums and balloon mortgages. His is truly an endangered existence.

Naiveté will be his undoing. He knows little of the wilderness that stands before him, an environment so hostile that his only choices are to adapt or die. If he is to survive, he must either make peace with or fend off the many scavengers who will come to pick his wallet clean.

His will be no easy adventure. He can be certain only of one thing: He will ultimately choose to live near a place that cashes personal checks on weekends.

1

The Day the Rabbit Died

"We make our fortunes and we call them fate."
   Benjamin Disraeli

*"So I says to the old lady, 'What the hell do ya think
they make foam for?'"*
   Toledo cabbie

It's the end of another day in your corner office suite.
Time to strut your expensively dressed bod out to the
Saab and head uptown to your luxury loft apartment. Your
secretary bids you good-night, and you suspect that she
secretly longs for you, to be in your world of fast cars, posh
nightclubs and conspicuous consumption. You have, on
occasion, heard the guys in sales whispering speculations
about your income, your weekends and your wife. And you
love every bit of it. You take to heart all of those beer
commercials you grew up on. Yes, you only go around once
in life, and now you're grabbing more than your share of
the gusto.

You get outside. The sun is setting over suburbia, cast-
ing orange hues that seem to come straight out of a four-
color Lowenbrau ad. The air has a certain feel to it. Yes,
that's it—there's a hint of Dover sole and white wine
ambience there. But alas, breathe deeply that happy-hour

air. Take a final luxuriating feel of your leather car uphol-stery. Turn up your nose one last time to that place where the expressway ends, that land of shopping malls and tract housing known as suburbia. For though you don't know it, you poor slob, somewhere a rabbit is writhing in the final throes of death.

SURPRISE! YOU'RE GOING TO BE A FATHER.

You pass through the usual stages. Denial. ("It can't be me. Don't you remember, dear? I was in Amarillo that week.") Anger. ("I DON'T WANNA STATION WAGON. I WANNA KEEP MY SAAB, DO YOU HEAR ME?") And finally, acceptance. ("Yup, the raised ranch is fine with me. We can put the swing set right there next to the pink flamingos.")

The Immediate Picture

If you're like many males, you may react in a peculiar fashion to the news of suddenly being made an expectant father. You may find yourself doing silly things like bring-ing treats into the office and screaming, "I'm-gonna-be-a-daddy! I'm-gonna- be-a-daddy!" You may attempt to make yourself look older by taking up pipe smoking or growing facial hair. However, this phase of the expectant father's new life lasts only about two and a half days. Then, for some strange physiological reason, nature returns his fac-ulties of logic and reason.

It's at this point that you notice that a good deal of office esteem has been lost since you made the announcement. Older male co-workers react with, "Jesus Lord, you did what?" These men are almost always fathers already, and they know what lies ahead in your now pathetic future. Your secretary, who once looked at you as though you were Cary Grant in the nude, now only mutters to you under her breath and avoids making eye contact. Why this sudden change? Because now she can only see a tired sap who will be dragged from Cub Scouts to Indian Princesses, and who will be dowdy and sticky for nearly the next two decades. In her eyes, your role as executive sex object, slayer of budgets and employee bargaining, wrangler of expensive turbo-charged Scandinavian autos, is over, dead, kaput, *finis*.

At home the immediate picture is little better. Your wife, a successful, savvy, beautiful person in her own right, has suddenly traded in her gray matter for Jell-O. The woman who once read Camus in the original is now needlepointing a tap-dancing rabbit and quoting Dr. Lendon Smith in the original. No longer does she browse through the market reports. Instead she browses through the market, buying a bonnet here and some petroleum jelly there.

Alienated at the office and at home, you begin to feel about as welcome as a window peeper in a Girl Scout camp. But the bad news is that your life will not revert back at gestation's end.

The Big Picture and Beyond

As the months of pregnancy turn into years of childhood, you are likely to experience strange alterations in your personality and behavior. This fatherly behavior is very similar to the behavior you noticed from the dorks and nerds of your high school years. In fact, scientists now believe that high school dorks and nerds are simply extremely mature adolescents acting out fatherly roles well in advance of their years.

You may, for instance, take a liking to wearing white socks with wing tips. You may feel like mixing stripes with plaids, or wearing a sequined T-shirt that reads SUPER

DAD. Your once hearty laugh may turn into a wheezing guffaw, and you'll find yourself laughing immaturely at inopportune times.

> Client/Customer: Pardon me, but could you direct me to
> the restroom?
> Employee/Father: TEE-hee-hee-hee-hee. Uh, yeah . . .
> tee-hee-hee, twitter-twitter-snort-
> snort . . . right over there, HA-HA-
> HA-HA-HA-HA, hoo-hoo-hoo-hoo-
> hoo-hoo.

Even worse, you'll have to control strange desires to do things like pack up the wife and kids and drive six thousand miles to see the world's largest loaf of zucchini bread. You may feel an uncontrollable urge to place a miniature Dutch windmill next to your rose bushes or sit in a webbed lawn chair out by your cul-de-sac and watch cars turn around as they search for a through street.

You could start to say things like, "Well, I'll be," and "She's gonna be a scorcher today, boy." What's worse is that you may lose your communication skills altogether as you learn to dispense with words and acknowledge your neighbors with a various assortment of nods and hand gestures.

All right, so the picture is pretty bleak. But c'mon, face it. Television has been warning you for years that this is what it was going to be like. (But did you listen? NoooooooOOOOOOOO. Conan here had to have sex at three o'clock in the morning.) Did you ever once see an imported beer commercial with a kid in it? Did they ever drag out a BMW with a couple of carseats in the back? Did they ever show a guy in a Ralph Lauren shirt burping a baby? Did Grandpa Walton tramp around the Appalachians in Sperry Topsiders?

Good-bye, luxury.
So long, spontaneity.
Hi there, Pops!

2

Morning Sickness

The human body is one of the most amazing mechanisms in the known universe, or at least that's what they told you in high school hygiene class. And if you're still buying into that line, you probably think you'll live to collect Social Security, too.

Don't believe me? Well then, consider just how well the human body adapts to oncoming motherhood. Before the rabbit's even cold, the woman's body goes on a kind of pregnancy alert, not unlike all of those World War II movies that had submarines preparing to dive . . . except no one yells, "Down periscope!"

> "We have egg penetration. Repeat. Egg penetration. All hands, prepare for puke mode . . . .
> Prepare for puke mode."

Such a scenario is repeated several times daily for at least the first trimester of pregnancy. Yes, the body is truly amazing. Give it a fairly commonplace task like assembling an infant—no big press, within the next nine months is fine—and like an executive after a pepperoni pizza, it starts sending out signals to stock up on Maalox. No, the body just doesn't have the right stuff. It's just no good in a crisis.

Suffice to say that morning sickness—from the Greek, meaning to barf or feel like barfing during delicate social situations—is something like a three-month hangover. Or to use a more meaningful analogy (They work for Ronald Reagan, don't they?), if you traveled to Lynchburg, Tennessee, and drained the Jack Daniels distillery all by yourself, you would attain something akin to morning sickness. The major differences are that morning sickness does not take away your eyesight or inflict harm on your liver. But everything else is the same.

What does this mean for the expectant father? It means that even though he won't be dashing from the dinner table to the porcelain, his entire world will be temporarily turned upside down. He'll know this alteration in his life is going to take place when, while sitting across the breakfast table from her one morning, his wife turns as green as an army barracks. Her eyes will have a listless carp-like daze to them, and the sight of dry toast will turn her stomach.

The father who is newly expectant will at first venture into mild hysteria . . . ("Stay where you are, honey. I'm calling the Mayo Clinic."). However, soon he realizes that morning sickness is about as regular as "The Today Show." In fact, his wife will probably lose last night's supper right after Willard Scott's national forecast.

Willard: And here's what's happening in your world this
    morning . . .
Wife: hhhhhhEEEEEEEEEEEEEEEEEEEEAVE

Before long, husband will be asking wife to grab the
cream and sugar on her way back from the john. Life goes
on.

Barely.

Morning sickness takes an insurmountable toll on home
and social life. During this period of time, many husbands
become accustomed to cooking family meals, since it's usually the only way they get prepared. Fathers should guard
against fixing any meal that's too elaborate because the
sight of even Chateaubriand will send their wives gagging.
And when husbands end up giving a thirty-dollar piece of
meat to the dog, *they* begin gagging.

Morning sickness affects the mood of the boudoir, as
well. The unfortunate husband who feels amorous pangs
during the morning sickness period is about as welcome in
his bedroom as a drag queen at a USO show. Any advance
is likely to earn him a sharp "Stay back or I'll throw up. I'm
warning you."

Of course, all expectant fathers have different ways of
coping with diminished sex. However, those who find
themselves watching *Barbarella* or leafing repeatedly
through the girdle section of the Sears catalog should seek
professional help.

As far as social life is concerned, morning sickness has
approximately the same effect as saltpeter. After awhile
there's no reason to go anywhere, and you no longer care
anyway. The husband who drives a few times to faraway
restaurants only to turn around in the parking lot and race
home so his wife can retch is soon satisfied with frozen
Salisbury steak and "The Honeymooners."

Husbands who cannot reconcile themselves to this fate, and to giving up contact with the outer world, often risk damaging their marriage. Some have been known to sneak off in the car after the wife is in bed so that they can cruise restaurant row yelling, "Hey, lemme see your prime rib. C'mon just a peek," and "Wow! Would you look at the Idahos on that plate." Those husbands who become too great a nuisance can be picked up by the local authorities and forced to endure embarrassing line-ups, fingerprinting and other degradations. Such a predicament may damage a home life, social ties and future employment.

Similarly destructive are the fathers who stay at home and brood. These men are often dangerous to themselves since they seek to destroy that which put them in this situation. Thus, stories of hobby shop vasectomies run high among members of this group.

Those who can look morning sickness straight in the eye, however, and say, "Go ahead, take away my restaurants and my friends. Tie me here at home with frozen corn and 'Gilligan's Island.' I can take that and more," are going to weather the problem nicely.

Though morning sickness ends at different times for all women, the expectant father will know when the ordeal is finally over because his wife will begin eating anything and everything in sight. Since she will want to pillage fast food restaurants on a nightly basis, the couple's social life returns at this time. However, the embarrassment of sitting in public view with a fat woman pawing frantically at a Filet-O-Fish sandwich often carries with it such trauma for the husband that he will, ironically, begin to wax nostalgic about the period of morning sickness.

Indeed, grocery bills begin to skyrocket at this time, and, perhaps most tragic, the couple's communication begins to break down—mainly because it's difficult for the expectant mother to talk with a mouthful of Cheetos. However, this enormous appetite will, too, begin to slow. Nature, which has planned for everything, automatically diminishes the woman's hunger drive as her bodily dimensions begin to resemble those of Hulk Hogan's. Yes, the human body is truly amazing.

3

Delivery Isn't Spelled UPS

One of modern man's most horrific traumas is the very recent expectation that he be present in the delivery room. Little more than a decade ago, most men could still get through childbirth by feigning concern in the waiting room (usually done by pacing) and subsequently passing out cigars. In earlier periods of human history, men were not expected to come anywhere near a woman screaming out the agonies of childbirth. Even cave pictographs show that prehistoric man would rather wrestle a saber-toothed tiger than tell his mate to do something insipid like breathe in and breathe out. Supporting this hypothesis, one set of cave etchings discovered in southern France has been interpreted as "Wife scream. Kid come. Me go out with guys."

But modern man has not fared so well. This poor schmuck is pressed into service (only a masochist would volunteer) and is made to stand next to wife and doctor so that he may feel about as useful as a Gideon Bible at a Shriner's convention. He is expected to "coach" his wife in order to regulate her breathing and keep her calm. They tell this to a guy who is screaming uncontrollably himself and for whom the word "coach" implies getting a man from first to second base. Still, ever the good soldier, the father, (oops—make that "birthing partner") goes through with his grisly task.

Too cynical perhaps? Listen, only civil service employees have less to do than a father in the delivery room. First, about all he's been taught to do is help his wife breathe. This is akin to trying to soak up the ocean with a Handi Wipe. His wife doesn't want to breathe. Her brain is sending signals to her respiratory system that say, "This is it. You're going to die. Better gulp plenty of air, kiddo." The effect of this is that when the expectant father coos to his wife, "Everything's OK, honey. Just breathe slowly . . . in . . . out . . . in . . . out," she says, "I HOPE A 747 FALLS OUT OF THE SKY AND KILLS YOUR ASS, YOU ROTTEN, SCUM-EATING SON-OF-A-BITCH."

But the father has been taught well. "C'mon sweetheart . . . in . . . out . . . in . . . out . . . I love you, my little Hostess Twinkie."

"SHOVE IT, SEX MANIAC. IF I LIVE THROUGH THIS I SWEAR TO GOD I'M GOING TO SPRAY OVEN CLEANER IN YOUR ATHLETIC SUPPORTER. I'M GOING TO NEUTER YOU WITH A DULL PAIR OF TIN SNIPS. . . . YOU'RE DEAD MEAT, BROTHER . . . DEAD MEAT, HEAR ME?"

"Now, now, my little Ho-Ho. You don't mean that. I know."

She does mean it—every last word. But only a few of the most honest fathers will dare admit that during such a verbal barrage they're thinking, Just give me a heavy object, and I'll be on the golf course in twenty minutes.

One way for the father to get through his grueling role as birthing "coach" is to take the term literally. If they want a coach, give 'em Casey Stengel. Better yet, Billy Martin. The assertive father will make a place for himself in the delivery room. Enough of this standing to the side and out of the way. He should position himself smack dab in front of where the action is and scream, "SLIDE . . . SLIDE, DAMN YOU . . . SLIDE!"

Even better, he can rush the whole process along by coaxing his wife in much the same way the opposing team taunts the batter.

> "AAyyyy, batta-batta. AAyyyy, batta-batta-batta . . .
> NO HIT-NO HIT . . . SWING!"

The husband who doesn't wish to take the adversarial approach can talk his wife through the delivery. It may also help if she's given a chaw of tobacco to give the event a kind of Nellie Fox feel.

> "OK, babe. Man on first and third. Bottom of the ninth. You gotta drive Gonzalez in. . . . Good eye, good eye."

While these coaching techniques are a good deal more helpful than the stuff taught in childbirth classes, they are often difficult for the father to shake once birth occurs. And it can be considerably embarrassing for him when relatives are contacted and he says something like, "I think we played a damn good game. We got off to a slow start, but our hitting came back in the sixth. I'm confident that this momentum will carry us into the play-offs."

Sometimes a father is lucky enough to stumble into a Caesarean section, which, of course, means that he doesn't have to do a damned thing but hang around the lounge. Shucky darns. No blood, no screaming and swearing, no funny doctor clothes. All the father has to do in this fortuitous situation is drop to his knees and give thanks to his maker, grab a cup of free java, prop up the feet and watch a little TV, right?

Wrong. Nature has imbued fathers with guilt that, at such times, comes to the surface—feelings that make him weak and helpless. Not only won't he be able to enjoy any of the freebies given to expectant fathers, but he'll have to work hard to suppress such thoughts as, What if my daughter grows up to look like Dom DeLuise? Once the father has slipped this far into thought, his mind will race and conjure up a number of other horrifying questions:

- How much does summer camp cost?
- Does the government supply oboe lessons to children who can show need?
- Are there special classrooms for children of hysterical fathers?
- What if my baby is allergic to me?
- Is the Sorbonne a good school?
- Does Princeton have a cheap extension campus?
- What if my son grows up to be a florist?
- Will my children stick me in a home for terminally interfering fathers?
- If my kid is a genius, will he refer to me as "the dummy"?
- What if I lose my job and can't afford MTV?
- Will I be known in the neighborhood as the Ward Cleaver who went bad?

- Will I live to see grandchildren, and if so, will I have to support *them*, too?
- Does our TV get "Sesame Street"?
- Will I be expected to actually wear what I'm given for Father's Day?
- Will I ever eat steak again?
- Will anyone find out that I thought Dr. Spock was Leonard Nimoy?
- Is there a special hell for fathers who refused to pay for computer camp?
- Will I be forced to wear a cardigan sweater just like Ozzie Nelson?
- Can I get the marriage annulled?
- How much do plastic slipcovers cost?
- Would it be rude to ignore the kid until it can dress itself?
- Do high schools still make grown men endure Dad 'n Daughter Datenight?
- How long is Little League season?
- Is there a God, and if so, do I have sufficient pull to get me out of this mess?

4

Fifteen Things Almost as Bad as Watching Childbirth

"Horror and moral terror are your friends."

Apocalypse Now

"Huh?... ooooh! YUCK!"

Anonymous father

Some human experiences are so terrifying, so absolutely incompatible with what we as civilized individuals know to be right, that they forever scar our psyches. Childbirth is such a thing. No doubt nature intentionally made the act as loud, sweaty and gooey as possible in order to send the male of the species running and screaming so that the female, who has reconciled herself to such moments of incomprehensible pain, may get the job done.

Until women began to believe that men should be made to suffer through childbirth experiences as well, about all the average man ever got to see that could be categorized as truly gruesome was a badly mashed raccoon on the highway. A badly mashed raccoon, however, cannot begin to compare with the horrors of the dread delivery room. For purposes of decorum, we shall not attempt to describe the blood, the pain, the cursing or the complete breakdown in communication that occurs at that time between the husband and wife. Instead, the point can be better made if we bring to light those experiences that might be almost as bad as witnessing childbirth.

Naturally, the key word here is *almost*.

For most men the experiences of the maternity ward are so shocking that a good many never actually get over it. A few go on to develop symptoms that are more reminiscent of shell-shock victims. Some fathers only experience an occasional flashback, the kind that comes on suddenly, causing them to crawl under the coffee table and whimper, "The contractions . . . I can hear them in my head."

Others are so shaken from the childbirth trauma that they must be forcibly removed from everyday society. These few are placed in specialized institutions where their needs may be cared for. Those suffering from what is known as "Post-Childbirth Shock Syndrome" live together in communes far from the cities that house the trappings of fatherhood. Most spend their days tending small gardens and receiving regular electroshock treatments.

A few sufferers have actually been rehabilitated to the point where they can enter into society for short periods of time again. Those who have successfully taken the long road back to recovery have done so only through intensive "Reidentification Therapy," a process whereby men are "reconnected" to the stereotypical male/father role by acting out behavior usually thought of as typical of many men. A daily regimen may include drinking beer to excess, reading *Field and Stream*, cussing, telling jokes about country girls and working with power tools. While eighty percent of those given the therapy can return to society at some point, most are extremely obnoxious and have few friends.

It is plain that childbirth is only for the stouthearted.

For those who wish to better gauge the intensity of this nearly intolerable experience, let us look at a number of situations that are almost, but not quite, as bad as watching childbirth.

1. The Spanish Inquisition (Note: Some items in the list may be harsher than others, but belong here just the same.)
2. Coaching Little League *
3. Preparing any recipe that calls for liver
4. Being told how much clarinet lessons cost
5. Attending a clarinet recital and realizing that all that money could have gone to undercoat the station wagon
6. An influenza epidemic **
7. Canned hash (Note: Most canned meats will qualify.)
8. A Buster Crabbe film festival
9. Learning in the spring that an overweight opossum got stuck in your chimney in the fall
10. That first realization that children's gym shoes cost about the same as leather wing tips
11. Any school talent show that involves yodeling
12. The pang of guilt you feel after you throw your old refrigerator out for the trash and you momentarily toy with the notion of leaving the door on

---

* Of the fifteen items in the list, notable authorities believe that coaching Little League is the only one that may qualify as actually *worse* than watching childbirth.

** Surveys show that a good many fathers would rather have their pick of a number of incapacitating diseases than be forced to enter the delivery room with a woman who is writhing in extreme pain.

13. Knowing the pediatrician and orthodontist so well that they call you by pet names
14. Taking your boss to lunch only to find out that the American Express card once in your wallet has been replaced with a wad of Silly Putty
15. Learning that some types of Tupperware can't be used in the microwave

Yes, the awful truth is that while childbirth may be a miracle, it is an icky miracle. There are, however, a few desperate ways to avoid watching childbirth. You may find that now is the right time to sign on for a stint with the merchant marine. Or you might choose to become a soldier of fortune (much neater than childbirth and the pay is good). Probably the most practical solution is plastic surgery and residence in a South American country. Your birthing partner will never find you there.

5

Naming Children

"A good name is rather to be chosen than great riches."

Proverbs 22:1

"I refuse to breastfeed anyone named Lester."

Anonymous mother

Perhaps the single most important task that an expectant parent performs is choosing a name. After all, a name will affect such future endeavors of the child as playing sports and meeting members of the opposite sex (It goes without saying that few people will date or have as a teammate someone by the name of Melvin), as well as signing bar tabs (Butch is a good name for this activity).

Therefore, the father will no doubt wish to pick a name that will afford his child every possible advantage. To aid him in this task, nature has generously endowed the father with a sharp and fertile memory, one that allows him to quickly search through his many years of experiences in order to cross-reference names with given situations.

For instance, in the case of naming daughters, most fathers will quickly decide that "Thelma" is, generally speaking, a bad choice for a girl. Of course, it's an especially bad choice for a boy, too. The father's finely honed gray matter tells him that since the name Thelma summons to mind images of a sweaty girl with glasses, large thighs and straight A's in home economics, it is unlikely that she'll ever attend the junior prom, or any prom for that matter.

A similarly negative choice would be the name "Sharleena" which, while a good deal more exotic than Thelma, conjures up visions of a kid who not only requests cosmetics and a garter belt for her tenth birthday, but who will, as she matures, develop the unseemly habit of flagging down truckers on the interstate.

A good safe name, on the other hand, is "Nancy" because it's rather neutral and does not recall any troublesome image. Besides, it's the name of a president's wife.

Get the idea now?

Where boys are concerned, both mother and father will wish to have ample input. The reason for this is that fathers are often overcome by a little-known gland that causes them to want to name their sons after athletes. Mothers, on the other hand, usually have the presence of mind to realize that very few bankers are named "Reggie," "Mean Joe" or "Bubba." But mothers can also be guilty of choosing inappropriate names. Wishing her child to have a name that will someday befit his lofty station, the mother may choose a name like "Emerson," "Winston" or "Sigmund."

At this point the father's memory will kick into overdrive and remind him of the many atrocities committed against members of his gender who were once unlucky enough to go to gym class with a name like "Emerson." Not wishing to bring up a son who will be mercilessly teased at nearly every school social gathering, the father will demand a different choice.

Such problems can be avoided by choosing "John" for a son. While a few of these men later regret having been named after restroom facilities, their numbers are so great that no one dares to make fun of them.

Often parents wish to assign names to their children that have special meaning. Girls, for instance, may be named for some culturally desirable trait. "Chastity" and "Faith" are examples. Further, girls may be named for the months in which they were born, such as "June," "April," etc. Similarly, boys will often be named after major religious and historical luminaries, which accounts for the great many boys named "Matthew," "Mark," "Luke," "John" and "Buzz Aldrin."

Parents are quite often compelled to label ("scar" may be a more accurate verb here) their offspring for a currently popular celebrity. While such an act may seem harmless, and even downright cute at the time, it has more serious ramifications later on, as others will surely ask such things as, " 'Spike Jones'? A family name is it?" The less tactful are apt to say something like, "Whaaaaat? 'Stevie Wonder Kosinski'? That's sure a dumb name for a girl." People can be very cruel at times.

As you can see, the danger in choosing the celebrity name is really twofold. First, most celebrities have silly names. Sylvester Stallone and Stubby Kaye are just two of the many examples. Secondly, few celebrities exhibit behavior that the well-meaning parent would want attributed to his child. (Historical Note: According to the last census, there were virtually no "Richard Pryors" listed as residing in Little Rock, Arkansas. However, there were forty-seven "Pat Boones.")

Of course, we can expect parents to go on naming children for celebrities and other icons as long as there are babies born (or until "Entertainment Tonight" is cancelled, whichever comes first). But many parents, unfortunately, find out only after the fact that some names will have serious negative effects on their children.

As a public service, a good many of these have been listed and categorized below:

NAMES THAT WILL SEND YOUR KID TO PRISON

Fast Eddie	Blade
Rocky	Rico
Big Al	Rollo
Vinnie	Snake
Sonny	Speed

NAMES THAT WILL GET YOUR KID BEAT UP IN PRISON (or almost anywhere)

Prudence	Bruce
Herschel	Homer
Cecil	Ayatollah
Wylie	Pinky
Hermann Goring	Penelope
Charles Manson	Seymour
Lucille Annabelle	Clyde

NAMES THAT WILL FORCE YOUR SON TO PUMP GAS *

Phil	Jake
Mac	Sam
Les	Gus

---

* Filling station attendants are almost always hired because their short names can easily fit on those little blue patches.

NAMES THAT WILL GET YOUR DAUGHTER PREGNANT BY THIRTEEN

Trixie	Brandi
Candy	Bambi
Fifi	Lola

NAMES THAT WILL GET YOUR SON INTO PROFESSIONAL WRESTLING

Crusher Calhoun	Grim Reaper Sullivan
Meatlocker Moe	Bomber Koznowski
Executioner	

CELEBRITY NAMES THAT WILL MAKE YOUR KID LOOK RIDICULOUS AND BRING HIM OR HER UNTOLD AMOUNTS OF SCORN

Minnie Pearl	Madonna
Mr. T	Too Tall Jones
Boy George	Tokyo Rose
Engelbert Humperdinck	Rip Torn
Eddie Rabbitt	Ozzie Nelson
Johnny Paycheck	Yogi Berra
Prince	

Part II

The Novice Father

He's a little bit Lewis and Clark and a little bit Rambo. He lives in a tortured, turbulent world. The last time he slept through the night was during the business trip to Albany. He has not eaten meat without soybean supplement since 1982. (Someone gave him a rib-eye in the office grab bag.) His house smells of formula and talcum . . . and worse.

He is the novice father, a tired, battered version of his former self, whose only wish is to be taken away some night by extraterrestrials or sent to prison for tax evasion. (It's no doubt quieter in both places.) In his spare moments he contemplates dark thoughts—throwing himself on a flaming hibachi, jumping into the septic tank, lying down in front of his rotary mower. Still, he has a mission. But his main problem is finding out what it is and how much it will finally cost him.

Part II

The Novice Path

6

How Babies Work

*"Marian . . . QUICK! . . . Little Billy . . . all over
the floor . . . the SMELL . . . aaaAAAHHHHH!"*

   Last words of an anonymous novice father

The known universe teems with amazing and inexplicable phenomena. So small is man in relation to the secrets and mechanizations of the cosmos, that he can do little but sit back and ponder over and over again the mulititude of questions that confront his species.

   Who or what, for instance, begat the lava lamp and what is that mysterious sludge that floats and bubbles within? Where does Velcro come from and how is it made? (Some believe that the stuff is mined in Peru.) And why are cab drivers always angry? Is it the result of a difference in their physiological make-up, or could it be that reading newspapers and eating pastrami all day in close quarters can radically alter one's personality?

   To these questions and many others, few firm answers are likely to be found. However, some headway has been made in recent years in terms of unlocking the mysteries that have long surrounded the functioning of babies. The reasons as to why babies do what they do have long per-plexed fathers. According to a new theory, our prehistoric forefathers, who had neither the capacity to reason in depth about babies nor the patience to listen to constant crying, would actually remove babies from the sanctuary of the cave in order to get a decent night's sleep. Stone Age fathers often, however, forgot about the dinosaurs outside, and the absence of the cave baby the following morning soon led to explanation through legend.

Believing that gods had come and taken their young-sters to a great camp in the Adirondacks, prehistoric fathers continued to make such child-care errors for another few thousand years. However, the extra sleep this ritual afforded is believed to have given early man the energy needed to later crawl forth from the muck and establish rudimentary social structures and shopping malls.

As late as the Renaissance, Leonardo da Vinci was attempting to understand the workings of babies. One of his earliest sketches is actually a process-drawing depict-ing what he believed were the four fundamental functions of a baby. These were incessant crying, eating, excreting and, one lesser known function, sleeping. The great artist and scientist worked a good part of his adult life trying to develop a method that would suppress the first three func-tions. Unable to come up with even one acceptable remedy, da Vinci later turned to developing the submarine and drawing naked adults.

Even in the twentieth century, great minds have obsessively pondered the intricacies of the infant, trying to understand how such a small organism can make such a loud noise. Few know, however, of preeminent physicist Albert Einstein's extensive work in probing the mysteries of baby mechanics. It is now believed that shortly before his death he was on the verge of cracking many of father-hood's long unsolved riddles. Unfortunately, almost all of his findings were lost when, during a reception after his funeral, Einstein's small nieces and nephews scribbled over his voluminous notes and computations with crayons.

Colleagues who have attempted to interpret his remaining work are sure that Einstein's studies of quantum mechanics and the Unified Field Theory were really nothing more than a "smoke screen" to conceal his life's work which revolved around the question, Why do babies sleep soundly during the day but insist on waking at 2 A.M. on a Sunday morning, when both parents have wanging hangovers? The answer still eludes modern man.

Today research is still being conducted in order to learn why babies do what they do. In fact, the U.S. government continues to study the elemental make-up and behavior of babies at a secret base in the desert southwest. But since no researcher worth his litmus paper wants to admit he's studying how babies work, all concerned prefer to remain anonymous. This keeps everybody happy. However, these researchers have brought extremely thought-provoking discoveries to light.

Consider. Scientists now believe that babies were actually meant to sleep nearly twenty-four hours a day until the age of eleven or twelve. The intervening stimuli which today cause infants to awaken about every four hours were brought about by our aforementioned neolithic ancestors who left babies outside the cave overnight. Essentially, the child of today wakes up at 2 A.M. because of a primal response to the fear of being eaten by a stegosaurus.

According to Dr. Leonard Schmitkin, a behaviorist at the Institute for Baby and Father Studies at Princeton, "In his subconscious state, every child suffers from the fear that his father will, at any time, chuck him out the door to become a meal for wild beasts. This also explains why, after a father enters a child's room, the youngster will stiffen up like a carp and play dead." Dr. Schmitkin believes that the sensitive father can help his child overcome what's now called Stegosaurus Anxiety by attempting not to grunt and swear in the middle of the night when his child calls out.

It is also known that nature has provided the infant with some rather ingenious defenses against the world about him. For instance, to discourage overfeeding by adults, a baby will instinctively open its mouth, once its appetite is satisfied, and let a mixture of strained foods dribble repulsively down the chin. The resulting sight leads the adult, whose instincts tell him or her to make loud gagging sounds, to put the baby food away and leave the room.

Similarly, to protect the infant from excessive jostling by relatives who might otherwise cause nerve as well as emotional damage, nature has imbued the young of the species with a special built-in defensive mechanism called the Projectile Puke Response. Not unlike the sting of a bee that's been angered, this response enables the baby to hold at bay insensitive uncles who delight in tossing the child. An instinctive reflex that elicits such responses as—"Holy Christ! . . . my tie . . ." and "Muriel, for God's sake do something!"—the Projectile Puke Response is normally very effective after only one incident, often keeping unwanted adults away until the child has reached his late teens.

Perhaps one of the most fascinating aspects of infant anatomy is the soft spot found on the top of the head. For many years doctors believed that this spot was an indication that the cranium had not completely sealed in order to allow for the rapid postnatal brain growth that occurs. Today experts believe that the spot's only purpose is to make the father feel excruciatingly uncomfortable and believe that even the slightest misstep will damage the spot, sending forth all kinds of gush and goo. Psychologists believe that Soft Spotophobia, more than any other reason, explains why fathers are usually so eager to buy the baby a football helmet and shoulder pads.

A good many physiological traits of babies are, interestingly enough, simply designed to make fathers go away. Since fathers, at least during prehistoric times, often exhibited negative childrearing habits, the baby's physiology had no other recourse but to adapt to its inhospitable surroundings. This need for adaptation is responsible for the development of the appendix, an organ that today has little purpose but to crowd even more the abdominal cavity and give doctors a reason to perform a couple thousand bucks worth of surgery. However, at one time the appendix served an important neurological function. Acting like an early warning signaling device, the appendix was capable of sensing when a father was in close proximity and sending such messages to the child's brain. Once the signal made its way through the body's elaborate labyrinth of nerves and synapses, it essentially told the brain, "Cool it! The old man's nearby, and we don't want to be a late night snack for some stegosaurus, OK?"

At this point a number of responses might take over. The baby might stop crying and instead giggle and coo in order to win the father's favor. The baby might also reflexively look in the direction of its mother and allow its lower lip to tremble. This was quite often a very effective response since it got the father in a good deal of trouble that haunted him for days.

Those babies who grew to adolescence, paleontologists believe, would later harbor great animosity toward the tribal fathers. One excavation has shown that it was sometimes the custom of young males to throw at least the smaller fathers into tar pits, stripping them first of all their worldly possessions. Sacrifices became such an integral part of the social structure during prehistoric times that this ritual has made itself manifest today in the form of college tuition and orthodontia fees.

According to archaeologist Dr. Otto Finsterwald, "With the disappearance of tar pits, later social groups had to find an effective means of ritually punishing its fathers. Toward this end, charge accounts and greatly overpriced services have worked very well."

7

Diapers: A Replacement Manual

Diapering is easily a father's most dreaded task. Men who have fought in the world's bloodiest wars, men who would think nothing of biting another man's ear off in a wrestling match, men who will clean fish while taking a lunch break—all are apt to faint at the sight of a truly foul diaper.

Some men have been known to change their names and addresses when expected to change a diaper. In some rarer instances, men will even take their own lives—usually by belly-flopping out an upstairs window onto the station wagon in the drive while screaming, "I'm not touching that thing, damn it! It's all yucky!"

Still, for the modern father, the father who wishes to avoid early divorce and the alimony and child-care payments that accompany it, diapering is a misery that must be endured. Toward this end, it is wise to remember that the mind is perhaps the most useful weapon to employ in diapering: It will repress the body's pain, even during this most severe trauma. That's why hard, seasoned fathers are able to escape the disgust and drudgery that comes with the diapering task. When changing the diaper of a screaming infant, they can practically will themselves to think only of some long-ago pleasant memory—a former girlfriend, a golf match won, a past convertible. When these men have do-do all over their thumbs and favorite tie, they actually can believe they are dropping a twenty-foot putt into the ninth hole.

The father must become familiar with the telltale symptoms exhibited by the child who's in need of a change. This aspect of diapering can be broken down into two main areas: leakage and aroma. A child who needs diapering is invariably damp. In addition, the child will turn almost everything around him into a wet mess if allowed to remain in this state. The carpet, furniture, walls, bedding, pets, stereo equipment, large appliances—all are subject to child dampness. Thus, the sooner the leakage is discovered and alleviated, the better for all concerned.

Easier to detect is aroma. Diapers have a scent all their own. It is sour. It is repugnant. It will gag a maggot; I guarantee. Some especially prolific fathers have been known to wake up screaming in the night, believing that they can smell a diaper nearby. This so-called Delayed Diaper Syndrome is now treatable thanks to funds raised over the years by telethons.

Diaper aroma has an important purpose, however. Nature, realizing that at some point in human evolution fathers would be tapped to help out in the nursery, is protecting the child against rash by alerting the father to the predicament. Think of it as nature's way of saying, "Hey, Pops! Better pull yourself away from that hockey game or there's gonna be a funk in here that'll curl your toes."

Nature's system works quite well. Most fathers, when presented with the diaper dilemma and its accompanying aroma, will either change the child's diaper or take a Greyhound out of state and live in anonymity for the rest of their lives.

Once the father has determined that the diaper needs changing, he must, unfortunately, actually change it. Some fathers have attempted to avoid the task by nurturing an ability to look in their wives' eyes and whimper, "Please, please, don't make me do it. I'll barf. I know I will. Please? Huh? Please?" This seldom works, however.

One of the great ironies of nature is that few children, no matter how messy, disgusting and foul their diapers, actually want to be changed. They will put up a bitter fight to keep the father from removing the offending diaper. They will scream, kick, bite and scratch in order to remain in their wretched state. Thus, the father must wrestle the child to the changing table.

At first, the father is likely to be surprised at the strength of the child. This newfound strength results from the fear of being changed and actually smelling like a respectable human being once again. No child wants that. The child will also exhibit an instinctive knowledge of wrestling holds. He or she will be able to break a half nelson with ease. An eye gouge or slam is often attempted by some children. And fathers must be particularly careful of the child who is adept at executing a sleeper hold. It is good for men to remember, however, that no matter how frustrating the grappling becomes, most states frown upon cage matches and tag wrestling between fathers and infants.

The best way to approach the child who needs changing is from behind. In this manner, an arm can be twisted up in back and the child can be pinned on the floor. The difficult part of the process is enabling oneself to reach clean diapers and powder while holding the child in this position. Several manufacturers are now marketing small infant straitjackets that allow for easy changing. If this manner of changing is chosen, the father should remember not to leave the straitjacket on for an extended period of time—even if he's watching the All-Star game.

The diapering father also should be aware of several hazards that can occur during the diaper change. The first, and perhaps the most abhorrent pitfall, involves the child who enjoys grabbing his own feces. Yes, as frighteningly bizarre as this sounds, it does happen. Some children are unashamed feces grabbers. They wait for the unsuspecting father to remove the used diaper and then they move in for the kill . . . with both hands. Needless to say, many a new polo shirt has been done in by the child who enjoys fondling his waste. The very best tactic for the father who finds himself in such a predicament is to dive for cover, as such children are also fond of flinging their feces. (Note: In the world of fatherhood, nothing is quite so feared as a feces flinger. He or she can take out clothing, furniture and wallpaper in the blink of an eye.)

If feces flinging gets especially nasty (here, the mind should roam free to conjure up various possibilities), the father should summon help—preferably a woman, since a majority are veterans in the feces flinging arena. If the father is alone in the house, he should have the decency to run from the house and warn neighbors. Something like, "Run for your lives! My kid's throwing poop at anything that moves." Some fathers caught in such a compromising position have been known to hide for days, even weeks, in heavily wooded areas near their homes as they wait for a mother (whose fortitude for such tasks is a good deal stronger) to come home and handle the aftermath.

The second common hazard of diapering involves baby boys. You guessed it! Some can even hit a dress shirt from seven or eight feet. Unlike the feces flinger, the infant boy who delights in acting like a garden hose gone berserk can be easily handled. The father must simply approach the diaperless child with some kind of shield. Usually the lid from a diaper pail will do. The father will resemble a cowardly gladiator, but in actuality that's what he is.

When the father has made it this far, it's a relatively simple matter (once a few wrestling holds have been applied) to position and attach the clean diaper. Though the father will feel a momentary sense of fulfillment, it is short-lived since the diaper is very likely to become soiled again within a matter of minutes, sometimes seconds.

In that event, there is little else to do but pray, pray for early potty training. For the less reverent, a handy potty training prayer has been made available:

> Oh Heavenly Creator, you who have chosen to humble men through the multitude of unspeakable parenting acts, make life more bearable by showing my child the way to the bathroom.
>
> Help our sons and daughters to disdain wet and soiled clothing, and lead them to desire to do their business in the privacy of restrooms.
>
> Help them to appreciate the expense of disposable diapers, and teach them the pleasures of wearing underwear.
>
> Let them know the shame of relieving themselves in public, and guide them in respecting the olfactory needs of their elders.

Fatherhood Is Not Pretty

Though our days of fathering are fraught with many miseries, we will be glad to overlook them if only, Father of fathers, you will bless our children with early bladder control. Amen.

8

The Miracle of Potty Training

To say that most fathers find diapers disgusting is sort of like saying that the Battle of the Little Bighorn was a bit stressful on General Custer. I know a lot of fathers who would sooner stick a foot under a mulching mower than confront the rigors of wresting an oozing diaper off the body of a screaming infant. This is precisely why fathers wait and pray for potty training.

Unfortunately, many first-time fathers suffer from the delusion that potty training simply occurs—like Christmas, the first frost or duck hunting season—that somehow the child will wake up, reach for a copy of *Sports Illustrated* and pad to the bathroom to evacuate his bladder and bowels like any other decent and respectable human being.

Sorry. It doesn't work that way.

Making pee-pee and doody is a lot like playing the banjo. Time, patience and practice in ample quantities are needed to acquire the skill. The father who embarks on his first days as an instructor of potty training will soon long for those simpler times of changing disposable diapers. During the transition from diapers to potty chair, the father will have to remain alert and quick. Like a presidential bodyguard, he must be ever watchful for child signs of strain, worry, dancing and intense grunting. And like the Secret Service agent, he springs into action when he's needed.

"EVERYBODY DOWN, HIT THE DIRT! I'VE GOTTA GET THIS KID TO THE POTTY, FAST."

In public places, most people will oblige, plastering themselves against walls so that the father may accomplish his mission.

"Make way folks. Let the man get his kid to the can."

If the father is successful in reaching the facilities in time, all soon returns to normal.

"Okay, folks, break it up. You can all go on home. The kid's all right. Just had to go number one." (Cheers and whistles from the crowd.)

Sometimes, however, a potty mission can go seriously awry. Case in point: I am at the K-Mart on a rainy Sunday. The day is important here, since Sundays, especially rainy ones for some reason, cause people to congregate in discount stores to while away the hours buying personal hygiene products. With me is my son. He is, at this stage, a novice restroom user. In other words, he knows when he's got to go, but he's about five years away from being able to reach the urinal by himself. So he needs my assistance. Besides, as our mothers told us early on, public bathrooms are known habitats for perverts and guys with tattoos. Thus, as a father, I'm required to act as bodyguard, nurse and valet to my two-year-old.

Sometimes, though, I'm his art critic. My son has a tendancy to interpret fecal shapes as animals, much the way some people see images in cloud formations. One time he saw a seal. Another time an elk. I hope it's a habit he outgrows. I have visions of him coming home from college and saying, "By the way, Father, the other day I made a Bactrian camel and a mongoose." At any rate, I've been instructed by his mother to offer words of encouragement at such moments. I say things like, "Man oh man, that's a great koala bear. Keep up the good work." While my actions may seem rather outlandish, I persist in order to ward off the consequences. No way do I want this kid to get discouraged and return to diapers.

Back to our story. Now experienced fathers will recognize that I've allowed myself to be put in a weakened position. First, I'm in a crowded store. Maneuvering to the john will be more difficult than usual, sort of like running an interception back eighty yards. Secondly, all kids like to try out new restrooms. My kid explores public lavatories the way Captain Kirk explored the Milky Way—going where no man has gone before gives him some kind of weird thrill.

On this particular day, my two-year-old starts to screw his face up. It's the first sign. Soon his contorted face takes him from cute to looking like Andy Devine with heartburn. I spring into action.

I grab my son around the waist and race down K-Mart's main aisle. I am rounding a display of plastic dinnerware when a rotund woman with a shopping cart rams me where it counts. I make sounds reminiscent of a walrus in heat, but continue on my mission. My son updates me on the status of his condition.

"Hurry, Daddy! I can't wait. I'm starting to make wet." (Note: Yes, making wet is precisely what you think it is.

But my wife and I think it's cute, and we've written this little nugget down in his scrapbook.) I am nearing linens when I finally spy the men's room.

"Hold on a little longer, kiddo," I yell. "Daddy's running for daylight now."

We get to the men's room door and my heart sinks. There is a sign: PLEASE ASK CLERK TO RING BUZZER.

I try to retain my composure, but I break down.

"JEESUS!" I sob, knowing that as time ticks away I stand an ever greater chance of becoming a human toilet. "Somebody help us. My kid's making wet AND THERE'S A GODDAMN BUZZER BLOCKING MY WAY."

I hear an electronic "buzzzzzzzz." My prayers are answered. An anonymous clerk from Layaway has taken mercy on us.

Alas, she's too late. I stand wet and dejected. Like the losing pitcher, the marathon runner who places second or the golfer who botches the putt, I have lost.

Sure, there'll be other days. But I wanted this one . . . for myself. We wander off in search of shaving cream.

9

The Feeding of Small Children

O ne of the great ironies of fatherhood is that feeding children, a task whose misery cannot be overstated, leads to more diaper changing. However, the ethics of fatherhood, as well as numerous state and federal laws, specify that children must be fed. This may come as some surprise to new fathers, but so will many of the adventures that make up fatherhood.

Baby food is one such adventure. While the father's first thought after initially encountering baby food is "I can't believe I once ate such slop," his second reaction usually concerns color ("Haven't I seen this in duck ponds?"). Baby food comes in three distinct but disgusting colors: orange, green and brownish gray. The latter is usually believed to contain some kind of strained meat, while orange and green denote mushy mixtures of vegetables that most children are known to hate.

The father can usually provide the child with a nutritionally balanced diet if he remembers to always serve a glop of orange, a glop of green and a glop of brownish gray. Giving the child these essential glops is really the easiest part of the feeding process. But here an important principle of feeding should be understood: What goes into the child as a glop usually comes out as a glop.

Getting glops of food into the child is the hard part. Though children will almost always be hungry at mealtime, they delight in playing hard-to-get. They expect parents to perform a series of feeding gymnastics before they will agree to open their little traps and scarf down any amount of orange, green or brownish gray. The first step in getting the child to eat is perfecting a good "wind-up" or approach to delivering the food to the mouth. Most fathers rely on something like, "NEEEEEOOOOOW . . . Open the hangar, here comes a plane . . . okay, open the hangar . . . neeeeeeOOOOOOW . . . C'MON, OPEN THE DAMN HANGAR!"

Other fathers will try to coax the child into eating with some variation of the plane/hangar approach. "Open up, here comes a cruise missile. . . . Better swallow the cruise missile before the commies take over the western hemisphere." Or, "Here's some yummy fossil fuel for my growing industrial power. Better gobble it up so your gross national product will get big and strong."

Occasionally, one runs across a child so ornery and determined to keep glop from entering his mouth that the only way possible to feed him is through sneak attack. This can usually be done by tricking the little bugger into laughing ("Look, Daddy's got pains in his chest.") Once the kid laughs, the glop can be rammed home.

No doubt the most humiliating part of the feeding process comes when the father is forced into mimicking the way food should be eaten. This usually means the father will rub his belly, pretend to eat glop off a spoon and say things like, "Oh, nummy, nummy, nummy. Me want some more. Me going to gobble this all gone," and proceed to roll about on the floor. Fathers who find themselves doing this are often justified in doing so, but they should make sure that all drapes are drawn and only close family members present. (WARNING: AT NO TIME SHOULD BABY FOOD ACTUALLY BE TASTED AND/OR INGESTED BY FATHERS. This stuff tastes like crap and will cause the feeding father to grimace and run for a beer in order to rid his mouth of the taste.)

The feeding of children involves a number of hazards that every father should be aware of. First, most fathers, realizing that feeding a child is definitely not as much fun as reading *Golf Digest*, will tend to feed children too quickly. They take advantage of the child's gaping orifice by shoveling as much food into it as they possibly can, hoping the kid will get full and go to sleep. On the contrary, the father who practices this shotgun approach to feeding can only hope to have the child barf on his penny loafers.

Even worse, the child may make choking sounds which anger the mother and cause the child to believe that the father cares more about Tom Watson than his offspring's own nutritional well-being. While this may be true, it should never be revealed to a child of tender years. (WARNING: CHILDREN TREATED IN THIS MANNER HAVE BEEN SHOWN TO BE THOSE PERSONS MOST LIKELY TO LATER SHOVE AGING PARENTS INTO A RETIREMENT VILLAGE.)

Another feeding hazard is dealing with the disgusting manner in which children normally eat—with their mouths open and with great sliding bits of spittle on their chins. The novice father will at first feel the need to upchuck at the sight, but like most, he will soon become hardened to it. Longtime fathers have been known to become so accustomed to the sight that some can actually eat a liverwurst sandwich in between spooning orange, green and brownish gray glop into their drooling little darlings.

One of the most destructive side effects of feeding is the nearly constant spray of chewed food bits that kids seem to generate. Most homes where several children have been raised will, under the scrutiny of magnification, reveal numerous layers of microscopic food particles on floor, walls and ceiling. Some fathers who wish to increase the resale value of their homes have been known to hose down all rooms and carefully brush the interior surfaces with Crest. (Hard to reach areas may need to be flossed.)

The most serious by-product of child feeding, though, is not the condition home or father are left in but the effect on the father's social life. Society, by and large, expects parents of small children to stay clear of restaurants, resorts and nearly anyplace where food is sold or consumed. While at first one might deem this attitude to be grossly unfair, more careful consideration reveals the practicality of keeping families with small children cloistered. Face it! Who can enjoy a $22.95 Surf & Turf while some highchaired refugee from a preschool is spraying strained beets through his nostrils?

Parents who venture into finer restaurants with small children are likely to receive the same reception afforded a leper convention. Such parents will receive the scorn of maitre d's and the frowns of fellow patrons as they announce their need for highchairs and booster seats. While mothers are often oblivious to the snickers, stares and revulsion of diners around them, and actually interpret the regurgitation of orange, green and brownish gray glop as a marvelous demonstration of nature's wonder, fathers tend to believe that such an act is all a part of God's plan to induce hypertension in males and whittle down the number of physically imperfect members of the species. They are also usually quite sensitive to the aforementioned snickers, stares and revulsion of diners around them, believing that somewhere in the room may be clients, business associates or former friends.

Unfortunately, there is little one can do to counteract this "untouchable" status forced upon fathers except to remember that eight to ten years spooning glop at mealtime is really not such a long time . . . at least by geological standards.

10

Thoughts to Ponder While Burping Babies

O ne of the first things that the new father will realize is that he will be forced to perform many fatherly tasks that are monotonous—stuff that would bore the hell out of a dead man. The father who is used to more cerebral stimulation than the spooning of green, orange and brown matter provides will soon notice that his mind may tend to wander. During a 2 A.M. feeding, his mind and soul may take a little trip to some long ago golf course. Or, he may opt to count the dots in the ceiling tiles of the family room while waiting for an air bubble to leave his nocturnal little schmuck. Such daydreaming is, of course, a self-defense mechanism that nature has generously bestowed upon fathers to keep their brains from turning to Cream of Wheat.

Indeed, the only way to survive the confines of fatherhood is to regularly run the gray matter through its paces, kind of like the way prisoners of war perform mathematical equations or run through baseball lineups to keep from going mad. Using fathers and prisoners of war in the same analogy is by no means simple coincidence. The two have a great deal in common, though the prisoner of war is not required to go grocery shopping. (The Geneva Convention does stand for something, after all.)

Fathers will find that the mind can be kept sharp if allowed to ponder the deeper philosophical questions that face modern fathers:

- Why is there no statue honoring the inventor of the disposable diaper? It is an accomplishment at least as great as that of the wheel or the frostless refrigerator. If it were not for this great individual of vision, our laundry rooms would still smell like interstate highway rest areas on an August day.

- If a father left his squalling kid in the forest without anyone else around and traveled miles to a roadhouse to down a couple of brews and shoot some pool, would the kid make a sound?

- Think about it. If aliens came during July and removed all the vacationing fathers to a distant planet, there wouldn't be any reason for children to scream, "When are we gonna get there?"

- If you locked your kid in a broom closet and forgot about him for a couple of months, what would the penalty be? And which would afford the best chance, a jury or bench trial?

- Why the big rush to name a kid before he leaves the hospital nursery? Why can't you wait ten or fifteen years to see what he looks like? Then if he comes home some day in a blue shirt with a tire gauge in the pocket, you can name him "Les" or "Butch."

- Isn't it rather silly to celebrate Father's Day by being with children? That's no holiday. Instead, how about drinks and dinner with a cute little bimbo named Sheila?

- Why is it you can wash forty-weight motor oil out of a sport shirt but not infant formula? The indelible properties of regurgitated formula would suggest that the transportation department could use barrels of the stuff to stripe highways.

- Who is the wretched vermin who decides that toys will be made of plastic, cost no less than twenty dollars, break before New Year's Eve, and not include a couple of D-cell batteries? If you find him, he's mine.

- Of all the various species of life on our planet, only the offspring of humans is so helpless at birth. Puppies are up and around soon after, as are colts and kittens. Only infant humans take their sweet time in the mobility department. However, once they're able to move about, they instictively crawl to the nearest television screen to leave sticky prints. Nature is truly amazing.

11

Fathers and Supermarkets

"Abandon all hope, ye who enter here."

    Dante

L ife is chock-full of humiliating little tasks, a seemingly basic principle upon which the universe was founded. But life's most horrifyingly gruesome act is that of supermarket shopping. This is particularly true for men in the early throes of fatherhood, who are used to a good deal more civility than this activity affords.

What makes a trip to the supermarket seem like a journey into the bowels of hell itself is the fact that it is an environment teeming with unspeakable acts, behavior so contrary to all we know to be honest and good as to repulse even the bravest and staunchest of men. In a sense, shopping is a kind of rite of reversal, where behavior that would normally get a person five to ten at San Quentin is accepted, and manners reinforced in polite society lead one to failure.

Therefore, the father who finds himself buying a week's worth of groceries for the first time, while the new mother is at home crying at the same rate as her colicky baby, must mentally prepare himself for the terror of that cruel place. It will be unlike anything he has experienced before. He will be faced with clerks meaner than his old master sergeant. He will jockey for a spot at the deli counter against customers who pilot shopping carts with the ferocity and deftness of a kamikaze. He will stand in lines that make the Seige of Leningrad seem like a fine way to kill some time. But when it's all said and done, he who survives the ordeal may hold his head high and call himself a man.

The gates of Supermarket Hell may be said to be the parking lot, where the mettle of those who would venture further is tested by dodging scattered shopping carts and broken glass. The parking lot is also a good place to observe another unexplained law of the universe: The Cart/Car Principle of Attraction. This law states that shopping carts and automobiles share magnetic properties, but how much varies depending on the age of the car. Few unmanned shopping carts are drawn to cars over five years of age. The opposite is true for new cars, though. They attract shopping carts from great distances, like bees to a hollyhock, and the more expensive the car the greater the number of carts and the greater the force at which they are flung. Though scientists are studying this phenomenon, the reasons for its occurrence are still unknown.

The father who navigates safely through the parking lot and actually gets inside the supermarket has but begun the battle. In the early phases of shopping, he must simultaneously steer clear of seasoned shoppers as they bull their carts down aisles and decipher a list of foodstuffs that has been prepared by his wife. Both activities are equally arduous. Steering through a torrent of weaving shopping carts demands concentration, courage and the reflexes of a cat crossing the freeway. At the same time, reading a shopping list that bears no order to the location of groceries within the store finds the father flitting from aisle to aisle, a jar of strained beets here, a package of processed artificial cheese food there.

Perhaps one of the most frustrating areas of the supermarket for the father is the produce section. Here he will be confronted by a myriad of loose fruits and vegetables, all needing to be pressed, smelled and squeezed in order to determine freshness. During this endeavor, there will be women nearby who can sniff out a day-old rutabaga at twenty paces. They have been blessed with genetic stuff that tells them just where to jab a cantaloupe and feel an avocado. The father, whose genetic stuff tells him how to add forty-weight oil to a '68 Fairlane, is clearly at a disadvantage. His best tactic is to find an obscure corner of the produce department and press and feel on his own, so as to make his ineptitude in the produce arena less conspicuous.

Where most fathers inevitably fail is the household cleaning products aisle. Since a good many fathers believe that paper towel dispensers somehow rejuvenate themselves and that elves enter the house late at night bearing new rolls of toilet paper, many are unaware of the existence of this aisle in the store. Since the only familiar product to the father in this aisle is Kiwi shoe polish, he is likely to seem dazed, wandering into shelves and items like a bat out in daylight. Such frustration has reduced some men to tears, and sobs of "I just can't find the two-ply tissue . . . oh, God! Please . . . won't somebody help me find the two-ply?" are not uncommon. The resourceful father will go and stand by the floor wax and wait for an elderly woman who knows the ropes to rescue him.

The climax of supermarket battle comes when a checkout aisle must be found. Here another strange law of the physical universe takes over: The Inverse Checkout Principle. If one has two items to purchase, there will always be a shopper with a month's worth of groceries in front of him. If, however, one has a shopping cart brimming with inventory and a screaming child hanging from the buggy, he will be stuck behind a person with two items paying by check and without a driver's license. I told you it was a strange law.

Before securing a position in an acceptably short line, the father will find himself locked in shopping cart combat with others who would like to get the hell out of this place. The deadliest combatants are extremely obese women whose sole purpose in the supermarket setting seems to be that of taking up vast amounts of space by lingering in lines that allow easy access to tabloid newspapers. Once the father has managed to navigate past individuals scrounging for their horoscopes, all that's left is standing in line for a sufficiently onerous amount of time to pay for his goods. But this brings us to one more irritating law of nature sometimes called the Short Line Factor. This law states that if finding a spot at the checkout is not a knockdown, drag-out test of endurance, then there is no doubt that a small sign has been overlooked, the one that says TEN ITEMS OR LESS.

12

The Child-proof House

Two popular theories exist about the best way to deal with small children and property. The first, appropriately called the Nagasaki Scenario, takes a rather fatalistic view of domesticated life. It dictates that children and destruction go hand in hand, that there is no way possible of adequately protecting furnishings, dishes, linen, tile and dry wall. In what is a sort of Skinnerian perspective, the scenario maintains that children simply happen, are a part of the environment, and that one must accept the inevitable household abuse that accompanies them.

Those parents who subscribe to the Nagasaki Scenario live in chaos. Their decor can only be described as Early Bomb Crater. Such luxuries as intact wallpaper, working plumbing and door knobs that aren't sticky are sorely missing from their lives. They have, however, reconciled themselves to such living conditions. Still, some Nagasaki

Scenario parents are eventually affected by their situation and can often be seen cowering and whimpering behind draperies.

There is, though, a small sect of stouthearted parents, mostly fathers with prior military training, who refuse to succumb to the baser acts of their children and who valiantly train and plot to combat their destructive strategies. These brave few, sometimes labeled Survivalists, are bound by a code of honor to resist efforts by their children to deface paneling, spill grape juice and nick end tables. They are desperate people who are not above taking similarly desperate measures.

The Survivalist's residence can be easily identified. For instance, not only is his home's exterior vinyl-sided but so is the interior. This preventative measure will ensure that walls can withstand an occasional head-on collision by a weaving tricycle.

Similarly, floors will be uncarpeted and designed of concrete that gently slopes toward an industrial-capacity drain. At the end of the day, father or mother can simply "straighten" the house by hosing down the rooms, washing away many hours' worth of milk, juice and cracker crumbs, as well as far more unsightly and aromatic substances.

Another nice feature of such homes is the bedroom area. Designed to suppress noise levels raised by screaming and pounding, the Survivalist's walls are a luscious twelve inches of insulated cinderblock, ensuring as well that once a child's steel-plated bedroom door is closed and locked for the night, parents can look forward to a sound sleep.

As the seasoned father will already know, one of the most destructive forces that can run amuck in his home is the child's young friends—friends in the same way that King Kong was a friend to Fay Wray. These "friends" can carve a path of destruction that would make a tornado seem like a beer belch. Once they are allowed a visit, nary a lamp, small appliance or screen door will survive unscathed. To prevent such atrocities, Survivalists will cash in the Christmas Club account to pay for a moat. Truly nice models come with an electric drawbridge that affords the father the opportunity to deny children outside of the family access at the touch of a button. To ensure against especially strong-willed children, the moat can be stocked with some type of predatory beast, such as piranha, crocodiles or insurance salesmen.

While some will worry that a drawbridge may be unsightly as well as a violation of local zoning, there are several easy ways to handle such matters. First, a moat can be attractively landscaped with evergreens around the perimeter. For those using a layer of barbed wire, as well, a privet hedge may be used. Secondly, in the event that a city inspector stops by to provide a hassle, the owner can quickly lift his bridge and scream through an open window, "I'm a father, damn it! Can't you fools understand that this is my only hope, my only salvation? And another thing, you'll never take me alive. Don't believe me? . . . Okay, Edyth. Load the howitzer."

The last item is particularly helpful in the event that the city inspector summons the SWAT team.

For the Suvivalist father, at least, one of the nicest features of his home will be his underground network of tunnels. With these helpful passageways, the father may slip off to a mid- week poker game, arrive home late with liquor on his breath and escape from in-laws without anyone the wiser.

Upscale Survivalist homes will even come equipped with a Doomsday device. In the event that fatherly pressures finally become too much, a sealed compartment near the sump pump can be opened by triggering an explosive hatch that houses a fake mustache, a false ID and enough money for airline passage to Venezuela.

13

Kids, Coats and Cars: A Strange and Terrible Saga

I can't be sure, but I think I'm becoming an agoraphobic, you know, one of those people who's afraid to go outside the house and who makes all kinds of excuses to stay in and watch daytime television. I read of one guy who hadn't been outside in twenty-eight years. He panicked at the thought of venturing beyond the front door. He simply holed up with his television and stayed put. Smart guy. Maybe a father. Of course, when you haven't taken the garbage out for twenty-eight years, the joint begins to get a little ripe. But just the same, one of these days I might be there right beside him.

It's just that going places with kids is a pain of major proportion. The time and preparation involved in getting a couple of kids in coats and hauling them and their sundry items to the car is roughly equivalent to launching a space shuttle, only you have more help in launching a space shuttle. When you stick the kids and their junk in the car, there aren't any little NASA technicians in white suits checking to see if everything's go. There's no one to offer support like—

> "Father One, this is Mission Control. Your car-seats are in position and ready for kid entry. . . . Diaper bag and stroller terrain vehicle are in cargo bay and functional. . . . All systems indicate go, over."

> "Mission Control, this is Father One. I'm registering some sticky crap on my brake pedal, over."

> "Father One, we read a Cracker Jack alert. Disengage foot. We'll delay during sticky crap removal, over."

It doesn't take a father very long to learn that leaving the house is not what it used to be. For those who have been fathers so long that they can't remember those days, leaving the house used to mean making decisions like, Should I leave the top up on the convertible? or Which tweed sport coat should I wear? Now do you recall? Leaving the house used to mean having to carry mirrored sunglasses *all the way* to the car. Back then spontaneity was also a part of your life, remember?

> Future mother: Boy, I sure could go for a corned beef
> sandwich.
> Future father: How 'bout that little place in Toledo? It's
> only six hours by interstate. C'mon, we'll
> be there by dawn.

Those days are gone now. Instead the father cringes at the mere mention of "shopping mall" (a derivative of the Latin *shoppingus mallus*, meaning "place where cash disappears") because he knows that he'll have to carry more stuff to the station wagon than Marco Polo took to the orient. For the novice father, leaving the house means extra diapers, extra outfits, extra food, extra bottles ("extra" is a key term in leaving the house). It means taking toys and strollers, maybe even a playpen. It means feeling like Jed Clampett every time he pulls out of the driveway.

No wonder that at the first utterance of "mall," "car" or even "out," the father will run like a thief, seeking sanctity beneath the utility tubs in the basement or hiding under leaves in a window well. Some have even been known to feign cardiac arrest and lie rigid on the floor of the den for hours. It seldom works, however. Mothers, the relentless, unforgiving taskmasters they are, usually pull the father out by his ears and point him in the direction of the station wagon.

Preparing children to go bye-bye is nasty business in any season, but winter is by far the worst. This is because small children wear mittens and boots, both of which were designed by sadistic garment manufacturers who relish the thought of fathers throughout the world cursing and tearing at their sideburns as they try to get these articles on small hands and feet. These same manufacturers also know that most fathers have large clumsy hands and perform tasks no more delicate than screwing on an occasional oil filter. So it is that most fathers put up with a good twenty minutes of wrestling boots onto feet that refuse to bend and sliding onto hands mittens that always miss the thumb.

Kid preparation in winter also means applying layer upon layer of clothing so that the family can safely make the frigid trek from car to mall. This is especially important for families whose ancestors were not bright enough to settle in the Sunbelt. There are tales of Midwestern families that have been lost for days on the wind-swept parking lots of shopping malls. (Historical Note: Few are aware that the Donner party was lost after they decided to venture out to take advantage of a January white sale.)

Getting layers of winter clothing on a kid is much like wrapping a mummy, really. The major difference is, of course, that mummies wiggle a good deal less and, once mummification is complete, usually don't announce, "Daddy, I gotta go potty."

Summer has its problems, too, in terms of taking kids places. Sure, clothing isn't much of a problem. It's the interior of the car that's a problem. You see that's because all of the stuff that kids have been eating and dropping in the car during the winter—Cheerios, raisins, M&Ms, suckers, Milk Duds, crackers, granola bars, etc.—start to rot in the summer. The car's interior looks and smells something like a garbage scow. Let's face it. It's damned embarrassing to drive to church with cockroaches gagging and hurling themselves from your windows. They'd rather be mashed beneath your all-weather radials than remain in the backseat with the kids.

Novice fathers would be wise to learn from the experience of one of their brethren, if only to know what lies ahead. A rookie father from St. Paul had to be hospitalized after he opened the hatch on his wagon one hot July day and noticed that the upholstery seemed to be crawling. At first he ran down the driveway screaming, "My Pontiac's alive! Hide the women and children!" Then, believing he was suffering from a case of the DTs, he signed himself in for treatment.

Of course, it was a source of major amusement to the more experienced fathers in his neighborhood who realized early on that last winter's foodstuffs had simply begun to blossom once again in the backseat.

14

Fatherhood on Fifteen Bucks a Day

O ne of the first symptoms of fatherhood is a severe cash flow problem. Even before the blessed event occurs, the father will notice that almost overnight his wallet has become a good deal lighter. At first, there are maternity clothes to buy, obstetricians to pay and a nursery to decorate. In the immediate postnatal period, the hospital will demand its cut, as may the diaper service and pediatrician.

From there on it really gets rough. Births are seemingly sniffed out by every predatory salesperson for miles. They will goad, harangue and intimidate you into buying family portraits, parenting magazines and mass quantities of life insurance (Die tomorrow and your family will live like the Hunts; live and you drag them with you into unspeakable squalor).

In the beginning, too, the father suddenly finds out that those items that one would expect to be reasonably priced (formula, disposable diapers, etc.) are about the same price per volume as truffles. The father soon learns that for the amount of money his "new addition" is costing him per week, he could have one hell of a great Saturday night in Atlantic City.

And it doesn't end there.

As the child grows, so does his faculty for expending the old man's disposable income. Clothing is a big item. The father can expect to replace a child's wardrobe approximately every third week, as he or she will grow faster than mildew in a locker room. Another expense will invariably be the multitude of activities in which the child will participate. Unfortunately, these endeavors, such as ballet, accordion lessons, Pee-Wee football and French, have an extremely low yield return for the father. These are, for the most part, activities that will gobble up his dollars faster than a black hole, but will probably fail to produce a Baryshnikov, Walter Payton or even a Lawrence Welk.

As the years pass, there will be summer camp, braces, driver education (this one adds a quick six hundred dollars a year in premiums and a peptic ulcer), and ultimately college, all of which carry heavy price tags and exact immeasurable physical toll on the father. Thus, it is wise for the father to become accustomed to his newly found fiscal woes early on. The father who cuts household expenses to the bone and budgets his paycheck may actually survive the score of parenting years without even one eviction notification. However, this can only be accomplished if he is willing to do away with some of the luxuries that he has long taken for granted. For those who have not yet mastered the art of fatherly finances, the following tips could be of considerable importance.

PURCHASING FOOD

Starch is cheap. Meat and fruit are not. The father who plans on weathering the financial horrors of fatherhood should count on a couple of meatless decades. His meals will consist of lots of noodles and bread. However, he should be able to luxuriate in an occasional can of Spam.

How should the father entertain friends or business associates? Instead of having the Wozniaks over for ribs on the grill, the clever father will supplant cost-conscious Twinkies for the unaffordable meat.*

AVOIDING BILL COLLECTORS

A father cannot afford to fall prey to his creditors. Usually the people to whom he owes large sums of money will hire collection agencies to outfox the father. But some parties, such as the newspaper carrier, may show up at the door in person. The frugal father will handle the matter in this way:

(Father sends his kid to answer door while he hides behind drape.)

> Carrier: That'll be $192.73. Listen, I can't keep carrying you folks much longer. You sure you can't pay at least something?
>
> Kid: Oh . . . uh . . . I guess you didn't hear. You see my old man died last week and they accidentally buried him with his wallet. Yeah, talk about your rotten luck. My mom's pretty upset, too.

The father whose child is too young to fabricate such competent lies may wish to learn to throw his voice. In this

---

* Warning: Never attempt to grill Twinkies.

way, he can prop his child up at the door, hide behind the drapes and simulate a conversation with the visitor. This alternative demands a good deal more work, however, and the father may simply wish to hide behind stacks of old newspapers in the garage instead.

DEALING WITH MEDICAL EXPENSES

One of the most costly situations that confronts the father is the medical emergency. Even if his employer offers a comprehensive medical plan, he will often get nailed by a deductible. For the frugal father, health related matters must be handled at home. Few new fathers realize that almost any surgical procedure can be done with household utensils. Severe cuts, for instance, can be sutured with fishing line, while incisions can be quickly handled with a can opener, pocketknife or electric router.

At first, family members may vehemently protest the father's cost-saving medical measures. However, they will no doubt come around to his way of thinking once he explains that the money saved through his home surgical procedures will pay for next summer's trip to Knott's Berry Farm.**

CONSERVING FUEL AND ENERGY

An additional way for the father to hold expenses to a minimum is through energy conservation. Utility bills can quickly decimate the family budget through their seasonal fluctuations and spiraling costs. So feared is the winter gas bill, for instance, that some fathers choose to read it by

---

** The frugal father has no intention, of course, of spending money on a family vacation. This is simply a ploy to get spouse and kids to shut up while he patches their wounds.

holding it up to a mirror, rather than looking directly upon the dreaded balance.

But such bills needn't pose a serious problem if the father convinces his family to become energy conscious around the home. There is no need, for instance, to wash dishes every day and consume unnecessary water and electricity. Instead, dishes can simply be separated according to stain. Those plates with orange stains will be put aside and saved for the family's next meal of orange food. The same goes for green and brown stains. Using this technique, the father will find that he'll only need to expend energy on dishwashing every week or two.

The frugal father will want to make a small investment in a herd of goats before he ventures too far along on his quest to slash energy costs. Goats, he will soon find, are year-round energy-saving devices. In the summer they keep grass and shrubs neatly trimmed so that power needn't be wasted on mowers and hedge trimmers. And while these goats are munching and manicuring, they are also producing next winter's fuel in the form of goat chips, which can be used in the fireplace or furnace. And still goats can be put to further use on especially cold winter nights by letting them sleep with family members in bed or using them as convenient wraps while staying up late to read a good book.

There, of course, may be the problem of explaining to friends and neighbors the goatly aroma that will eventually permeate the family residence and surrounding area. After all, there is some embarrassment connected with the admission that twenty to thirty goats have moved in. However, such oders can easily be explained away if the father simply posts a sign on the front door warning that his home has been quarantined because residents are suffering from a highly contagious foot fungus. He will be bothered by few questions after taking this step.

While expenses can only be cut back so far, there are many other ways for the father to earn supplemental income. Feigning death for the life insurance, selling blood and claiming family pets as dependents are just a few easy ways to begin. Others such as counterfeiting and gunrunning require greater effort. Still, whatever strategy the father finally chooses, he will be rewarded in knowing that he's responsibly providing for his family's security and well-being.

Part III

The Well-Worn Father

You have seen his face—in a crowded subway, on a conjested highway, in the dairy aisle of the all-night grocery. He is creased, stooped and perhaps a little gray. He has at least a little paunch and more likely a roll around his middle resembling a steel-belted radial. He has the look of one who has been around, one who has traveled many times the secondary highways of life.

Yes, he's a father.

From the empty look in his eyes to the scuff marks on his discount shoes, he is every bit the part, a veteran of the cruelest side of domestic life. Do not look in his pockets; he has no money. Do not question him; he has no answers. Do not threaten him; he is defenseless.

He is a father, plain and simple, one with so much mileage that if he were a Pontiac, he would have been sold for scrap years ago.

15

Fathers Through the Ages

"Three birthdays in a row they gave me a leaf blower. A dog deserves better, I tell you."

Former father now living in Paraguay

The world is changing in many ways. While only those who have been living in a cave for the last thirty years or tucked away in remote parts of Wisconsin will proclaim that statement profound, it is, nevertheless, true and an appropriate starting point for discussion about the changing roles of fathers.

Face it! Just as cars with fins gave way to subcompacts and once stout-bodied beers have been emasculated by the removal of calories (where are today's great beer bellies, I ask you), so too have fathers gone through a sort of restyling. The once proud (though, granted, homely) beast who could lay waste to obnoxious anklebiters and call all of suburbia his very own is nearly as extinct as the passenger pigeon. In his place has risen a subspecies who is given to pleasantries and compromise, a whining organism who defies the laws of natural selection—a guy who will not only choose a white wine cooler in place of an imported

beer, but one who'll allow the television to be comman-
deered by those who would watch the "Frugal Gourmet"
instead of the play-offs.

SSSHeeeeeeez!

Fathers today perform many tasks that they once
believe to be well below their rightful position. (Historical
Note: More specifically, this was a reclining position on the
living room couch in front of a nineteen-inch Zenith while
chewing a mouthful of beer nuts.) Modern fathers have
been known to diaper babies, cook an entire meal and
drive daughters . . . DAUGHTERS! . . . to gymnastics.

On the contrary, all that was regularly expected from
the father of old was the expulsion of gas now and then. It
must have been grand, that long ago era—something like
Camelot perhaps.

(At this point, imagine that the page is getting wavy.
That's right, just like those cheap effects used to depict
dream sequences in the movies. Dissolve to next scene.)

I can see my own father coming home from work. He
walks through the kitchen door and proceeds straight for
the refrigerator. He knows it contains beer. Fathers of old,
legend has it, would only come home from work if they
knew there was beer in the fridge. A kind of sixth sense, a
"beer sense" if you will, allowed them to know whether or
not they should go straight home or head to the local
tavern for "a couple three short ones" with the fellas.

He cracks open a can and allows the mystical tonic to
begin its cleansing process, washing away the indignities
of rush hour traffic, middle managers and sack lunches.
All the while he does this, my mother pauses and watches.
She knows better than to speak during mid-beer gulp. She
understands the ritual and its importance in the family. It
is a sacred act . . . the Way of Beer and Pretzel.

Finally the can is exhausted and she dares to speak. "Little Ralph got into my sewing box and gave himself a haircut with the pinking shears today. . . . Lisa needs twenty-five dollars for tap-dancing shoes. . . . Timmy knocked another ball onto the Beldeckers' front porch and . . ."

"He get on base?" says my father.

"Who?" asks my mother.

"Timmy," my father replies. "Should at least get a double for pokin' one that far." He proceeds to read the evening paper.

"No, he fell over the Collins boy while running to first. Oh, and I forgot, he chipped his right front tooth in the process and cracked the frames on his glasses. And the ball hit Mrs. Beldecker's mother-in-law in the temple— she's visiting from Buffalo—and her hearing aid was knocked loose and fell into her iced tea. She wants $175 for a replacement right away."

My mother had struck a responsive chord. The only way to pull my father away from a newspaper, nap or Cubs double-header was to mention money. Even more effective was mentioning that he suddenly owed somebody money. After all, this was a man who had long ago taken it upon himself to enforce strict household conservation policies. He had been known to loosen light bulbs to prevent their accidental use, and occasionally he would track family members through the house, turning off the trail of lights they invariably left behind them. He had developed an acute sense of hearing that allowed him to know when the toilet paper roller in the bathroom had spun around one too many times, giving him cause to scream, "Jah-EEEEEses! Will you take it easy with that stuff? That's enough to keep the 101st Airborne stocked for a year."

99

No, my father did not look kindly on the prospect of owing a neigbor money.

"JahEEEEEses! Do they think I'm made of the stuff or what?"

"She says she'll sue if she has to," my mother warned.

My father, like most of the old-model fathers, never took kindly to a threat. And threats came in all kinds of forms. They weren't necessarily verbal. If a driver passed him in the right lane on the interstate, my father took this as an affront to his manhood.

"Look at that maniac go." (All other drivers were maniacs to my father.) "Goin' like a bat out of hell. Probably from Indiana." (To my father, the worst thing that could happen to a person was for him to be from Indiana, a place he believed to be a breeding ground for bad drivers because its desolation gave them little to live for.)

He would then proceed to give chase until he passed the said maniac and redeemed himself and the family name.

Threats could also be delivered in the subtle actions of nearby neighbors. When one year Mr. Beldecker threw out his Christmas tree and it landed well over on our property, my father, wearing only his undershirt and unsnapped trousers and with his face half-covered in shaving cream, ran straight out into the snow and tossed the offending tree back at Mr. Beldecker. A struggle of sorts ensued, a kind of tug-of-war with a dried-up balsam, but my father, larger than his opponent, succeeded in giving the tree a stout hurl right into the Beldeckers' plastic nativity scene, knocking Joseph into the Three Wise Men. Perhaps both paused expecting a lightning bolt, but soon the tattered balsam rested just over the Beldecker property line and a truce was called. However, as spite, Mr. Beldecker left the tree as a slowly decaying eyesore until mid-June, when finally some neighbor kids hauled the trunk away to use as a spear.

So my father was not about to take the threat of a lawsuit lightly, especially one from the Beldeckers. More serious was the fact that he'd been put into a compromising position with his arch nemesis by one of his own children. Perhaps the modern father would talk things over with his child, try to understand the circumstances that had led to the problem. Not my father. He wanted blood, vengeance.

Cursing filled the house, as well as promises of such unspeakable atrocities as curfews, increased chores and months, even years, of no allowance. He ranted. He stormed. He puffed himself up to full patriarchal grandeur. Like a lion protecting its territory, he was ready to strike. But more like the opossum, he would have to feign defeat first.

Later my father went over to the Beldeckers and paid for a new hearing aid. He made the customary apologies and then returned home. But he was not about to give in quite that easily. Frustrated by a family that had weakened his defenses and hungry for retribution, he waited all that night on the front porch for the Beldecker tomcat to mosey into our yard. For years the cat had interrupted my father's sleep and offended his sense of territoriality as it mated beneath his bedroom window and left its scent on the whitewalls of his cars. And now he was ready to pay the Beldeckers back. Armed with water balloons and a pellet gun, he lay in wait for the cat. My father had not caved in. He had picked up the gauntlet. And in the early morning hours he sat in the dark, silently musing about the Beldeckers' reaction when their wet and bruised feline returned home.

Ah, Camelot. What man does not long for those days when fathers were spared the degradations of feeding and diapering and could concentrate on the more dignified matters that were their rightful responsibilities? I doubt there is a man who would not gladly trade the mundane acts of modern fatherhood for just one good Christmas tree tug-of-war or cat attack.

16

Anatomy of a Father

L ots of things get better with age. Wine, if properly treated, improves with the passing of years. Penny loafers, the more they're worn, just keep getting better. And so it is with old blue jeans. Rum cake, too, up to a point. Even some European cars keep humming along a decade or two after the warranty has expired. But, alas, fathers, like cottage cheese and ripe bananas, only seem to quickly peak and embark on a long voyage of slow decline.*

The zenith of fatherhood occurs sometime during the first year. In the early months, the father coasts along in what can only be called a state of euphoria, one that is kindled by a rich fantasy life kept alive by images of his child becoming president, chief justice, a gold medalist or a game show host. But soon, as such tasks as diapering,

---

* In actuality, fathers have many more soft spots than bananas.

feeding and, most of all, supporting his child begin imping-
ing on his dreams, the father begrudgingly acknowledges
that probably the best he can shoot for is a plumbing
contractor. This jolt of reality is enormously sobering to
the father, and soon afterwards his spiritual well-being
begins to sour faster than potato salad at a Labor Day
picnic. The emotional energy evident at the start of
fatherhood crumbles somewhere between the sixth
straight week of sleepless nights and the first pair of
shoes, leaving only an ugly core of lethargy in its place.

Physically the father fares little better. After a few years
of assembling playground equipment, tripping over tricy-
cles and worrying about mounting bills, his body begins to
show the strains and excesses of fatherhood. As the years
pass (and the children grow from semicute to incredibly
obnoxious), his outward appearance will bear a remark-
able likeness to that of a retired salesman's sample case.
Stretched, dented, scratched and frayed, the father
exhibits the scars of his child-rearing years like so many
old bumper stickers.

Perhaps to better illustrate the unique physiology of the
journeyman father, we should take a closer look at those
parts of his anatomy that take the most abuse.

BACK

Like the mule and ox, the father is little more than a
beast of burden. After a full day of toiling in the office and
competing in rush hour traffic, the father can usually
expect to come home to the responsibilities of carrying out
the trash, providing horsey-back rides and rotating the
tires on the conversion van. Such activity takes an enormous toll on the father's back, little by little weakening
each of his pathetic vertebrae.

This, of course, explains why most seasoned fathers are at least slightly stooped—well, this and the fact that their spirits have been broken. Actually, the angle at which a father stoops is usually in direct proportion to the number of children and outstanding loans he has endured. One unofficial report tells of a man who, with seven kids, a second mortgage, two car payments and whole life insurance premiums, was bent at nearly a right angle. Only now is there a bill before Congress arguing for rights and benefits to bent fathers.

STOMACH

There is an obscure Bulgarian maxim that states, "A man who believes himself a father, but who exhibits not the abdominal bulges of fatherhood before his temples gray, can never call himself a man." Deep, those Bulgarians. A similar sentiment can be found in the culture of the Aborigine. Loosely translated, it goes, "He who can still fit into last year's loincloth is not a family man, nor should he be known as 'Pops.'" Many cultures have long idolized the fat of fatherhood, and to this day paunch remains a major side effect.

Today these paternal rolls of flab are so widespread that, in the jargon of the medical profession, they are known as "dads," stomach fat that at first hangs over the belt but can hang over the pockets in some cases, making it hard to retrieve car keys. The major reason for "dads" is poor nutrition. Burdened with the responsibility of paying for orthodontia and designer athletic wear, the father has little choice but to sacrifice his health and eat so-called junk food. Indeed, many fathers go years without tasting a porterhouse or a rib roast, subsisting instead on white bread and spaghetti from a can.

SCALP

One of the most troubled parts of the father's anatomy is the top of the head. Almost all fathers suffer from a certain amount of hair loss. This hair erosion may be as little as a slight thinning at the crown (that part of the head that can never be seen in a mirror, but which, when barren, can blind those around you on a sunny day) or as severe as near total loss. Most fathers, however, will retain at least a gruesome fringe that resembles the edges of those funny tablecloths that your grandmother used to put on everything.

Hair loss among fathers can usually be traced to children, either directly or indirectly. Children can directly cause this loss through the instinctive and extremely painful way in which they ride on the father's shoulders by grabbing fistfuls of hair and holding on as though they were reeling in a marlin. ** Observant fathers may have noticed that on occasion they will feel a shiver start at the base of the back and quickly rise to the shoulders. Scientists now believe that this reflex is simply a bodily response to bearing the weight of too many children. Essentially, the brain is telling the nerves along the spine, "Shake like hell, and maybe this little wretch will fall off on his head." Unfortunately, the child usually takes several clumps of hair with him.

The father also loses hair indirectly from children. However, it is usually the father who pulls it out as he blames his offspring for mounting bills, noise levels far in excess of the average human's pain threshold and Play-Doh in the shag carpeting.

** During the 1950s, children were forced to grab collars since most fathers had crew cuts. A more painful period occurred in the sixties and seventies when a good many fathers sported long sideburns.

NOSE

Less noticeable, but still a part of the father's anatomy that takes a beating, is the nose. From the day his child comes home from the hospital to the blessed occasion when his "pride and joy" shuffles off to college, the father's nose is constantly assailed by a barrage of terrifying smells. Most fathers actually believe that the smells go away when the child is about two years of age. This, however, is simply an olfactory illusion based on the fact that the father's nose has already begun to adjust to its fetid environment.

Once potty training has occurred, the father's nose must still deal with incidents of car sickness, unwashed gym clothes, sweaty hair and snacks that have been allowed to decay in the child's room. Unfortunately, in the event that the father accidentally sires a second child, the nose must become accustomed to infant-toddler smells all over again.

Some anthropologists have actually speculated that eventually the nose may disappear completely as a feature from the male face. Their belief is based on observable natural phenomena. As an analogy, one expert, Dr. Darryl Pinehurst, has offered this example: "It's like overfeeding a bowl of goldfish. Feed them seven or eight times a day and those little devils will be floating the next morning. The nose is much the same. Too many bad smells and KAPLOOHEY! . . . no nose." ***

Among the many species of life on our planet, the human male is perhaps the most enigmatic. Why does he take

***

*** Dr. Pinehurst is a nasal archaeologist who specializes in the noses of primitive peoples. His latest book, *In Search of Ancient Noses,* won him a research grant from the Association of Facial Tissue Manufacturers.

such physical abuse from those usually dependent upon him? How can his body continue to withstand the punishment that his offspring mete out? And why doesn't he change his name, clean out the savings account and leave the country with his secretary? Of the human male, we may never know the answers to these and other age-old questions.

17

Fathers and Sex Appeal

For some reason, in a rear view mirror I look a lot like Warren Beatty. All I have to do is scrunch down in the seat a little so my nose and mouth can't be seen, push my hair forward over a thin spot, don a pair of sunglasses, and WHAMMO, I'm a dead ringer for the guy, providing the shot of Warren Beatty is a kind of spaghetti western close-up between the cheekbones and the eyebrows.

Not that this resemblance is capable of generating any money, mind you, but there have been times when the talent has proved handy. One is when I've attempted to preserve some small appeal to the opposite sex, a task which seems to grow harder in proportion to the number of kids being hauled around in the back seat of my car. This is largely due to the trappings of fatherhood which muck up any attempt to project sophistication, charm or virility. It is damn difficult to look sophisticated, charming or virile while toting about playpens, toddlers, diaper bags and baby bottles in public view. Well-organized maybe, but never sophisticated, charming or virile.

This is where my Warren Beatty look comes into play. I use it as a kind of counterbalance to all the kiddie paraphernalia I'm loaded down with when I venture forth to the mall or restaurant. Listen, let me explain how this works, but remember that the Warren Beatty look shouldn't be practiced in the company of others. The less informed will only point and snicker. Actually, only an experienced father, or a dowdy single guy clutching vainly to youth and sexuality, should try this technique.

OK, picture this. You're out alone with the kids. Your wife is having her hair done, and your kids are in the back seat, latched like an Apollo crew into carseats. One sucks on a Lincoln Log; the other reaches forward to drive a "Dukes of Hazzard" racing car up the nape of your neck. You're on your way to the hardware store to buy plastic edging that will protect the corners of your walls from being nicked apart by indoor riding toys.

Now as you near the hardware store, you stop at a red light. You're minding your own business, listening to the farm report on the radio, when your well-worn wagon is suddenly flanked by a fire engine-red Maserati. Oh, you can handle the fact that there's a Maserati there and you're in something that looks like a prop for a Ma and Pa Kettle movie because you know that you'd never get the kids and all their gear into a Maserati. No sweat. You're not upset. After all, what good's a car that won't hold at least two carseats, a stroller or two, a playpen and two week's worth of formula and disposable diapers?

Naw, that Maserati doesn't bother you one lick. What bothers you is what is driving the Maserati—a girl with a head full of hair nearly as red as her car, a girl striking a majestic pose at the wheel, a girl who'd make Joe Namath stammer and twist his hair, a girl who is going to leave you and your virility in a cloud of dust once that light changes. Unless . . . yes, unless you can pull off one good Warren Beatty look, a look that says, "Listen, baby, I've seen it all and done it all. And I gave it all up for a seven-year-old station wagon, a couple of carseats and wet Lincoln Logs. And another thing . . . I'm so damned confident of my masculinity that I don't care if this kid in the back seat here runs a 'Dukes of Hazzard' racer up and down my neck, see."

You know the look, the one Warren used on Eva Marie Saint in *All Fall Down*, a look that both chills and sears the female sex. And now it's yours to use with wild abandon.

You scrunch down in the seat, shaking a lock of hair forward onto your forehead. Shaking a lock of hair forward is important because it gives you a kind of natural "Gee, I haven't had sex in nearly an hour" look that will help you cast off the image of staid family man.

Next, you drape your arm across the empty front passenger's seat (Just ignore that phantom sensation of feeling that your wife is there) and simultaneously put your sunglasses on. All that's left is for you to turn in the direction of the Maserati with the redhead and slouch. Slouching is a nice touch. We experienced fathers call this the "James Dean." It shows you really don't care . . . about anything . . . the side-molding dangling from your wagon, the Tupperware container of Cheerios that comes sailing into you from the back seat, the "Dukes of Hazzard" racer on your neck or the breeze that starts to move the lock of hair from your forehead back to its original spot beyond your receding hairline. Slouching can show a lot about a guy.

You turn to the girl, prepared to unleash upon her the full Warren Beatty look. She, however, is looking in the opposite direction, at a guy riding a Harley. He has long blond hair trailing out behind his turned-up collar, a tattoo of a scorpion on his upper arm and mirrored sunglasses. He's probably named Vince.

But you don't care. You're ready with your look—slouched, scrunched and ready to go. You touch the accelerator a little, revving the engine to drag her attention away from Vince. She turns. You LOOK. Suddenly, your wagon lurches forward and dies, barely missing a woman in the crosswalk who, in trying to save herself, drops a bag of tomatoes and calls you an idiot maniac.

The light changes and the girl and the Maserati barrel off down the street. The guy in back of you starts to honk and then finally tears past you on the left. He shouts something about moving a toilet. Finally it starts and you drive off, once again on a quest for plastic edging.

What happened? You were slouched, scrunched, coiffed and sunglassed, so where did you go wrong? That's right, never take your foot off the clutch while the car's in gear.

18

The Father as Second-Class Citizen

T he father suffers through a lifestyle that is distinctly different from other men, or those who can be categorized as non-fathers. Once a man enters into fatherhood, he must sacrifice a good deal more than two-door coupes and French restaurants. Indeed, a child in the home affects nearly every facet of male existence.

* * * *

Non-fathers carry something called cash. Fathers carry large numbers of credit cards.

Non-fathers buy on impulse, things like cashmere sweaters, motorcycles and imported beer. Fathers buy on time, things like cribs and playground equipment.

Non-fathers wear expensive Italian shoes. Fathers wear vinyl loafers that are made nowhere near Italy.

Non-fathers drive cars that hold the turns. Fathers drive cars that hold the kids.

Non-fathers fly to Switzerland. Fathers drive to Disneyland.

Non-fathers spend weekends taking in the theatre. Fathers spend weekends taking out the trash.

Non-fathers like to use their Sundays fixing brunch and Bloody Marys for six close friends. Fathers spend Sundays oiling training wheels, hitting the discount stores for sales on cornstarch, and waking up at exactly the same ungodly hour as they do on a weekday.

Non-fathers eat seafood quiche. Fathers eat macaroni and cheese . . . from the box.

Non-fathers play tennis. Fathers play pat-a-cake.

Non-fathers live in the fast lane. Fathers live in a subdivision near a good school, an all-night grocery, a clinic and a gas station.

Non-fathers wear silk ties with subtle designer logos. Fathers wear whatever they got last Father's Day, something in a palm tree, perhaps.

Non-fathers invest in certificates that mature in a year. Fathers invest in shoes for feet that mature in six weeks.

19

The Father's Library of Threats and Disparaging Remarks

One of the father's most onerous tasks will be that of maintaining some semblance of order in the home. For without order, respect and occasional moments of peace (these occur seldom and normally can be found only by locking the bathroom door), his surroundings are likely to take on the atmosphere of a K-Mart during a blue-light special.

In order to keep the peace, the father will call upon all of his resources—logic, fairness and faith in a Supreme Being. Unfortunately, none of these will get the job done. So the father will resort to the tactic that has served his forefathers so well—threatening.

In order to be effective, a threat must 1) dupe the child into believing that it can actually happen, and 2) be profoundly contrary to all that we know to be moral and decent. By devising a threat that assuredly will scare the bejesus out of a child, the father normally will not be put in the embarrassing postion of having to follow through on a ludicrous threat. In this event, however, the father may simply wish to say something like, "Well, I would stuff you in a sack and throw you in a quarry, but lucky for you I don't have the time right now."

Since threats are no small part of the father's home life, a collection of some that may be effective in various situations has been provided.

- Say, did I ever tell you about the thing that lives in the woods and feeds off the flesh of really bad kids? No? Well, I'll go get him—he's a friend of mine.
- Come out of that bathroom NOW! Okay, Margaret, send the naked baby pictures to the *New York Times*.
- One more time and your mother and I are going to hop on a jet to Vegas and blow your trust fund.
- Now in all the commotion, I can't remember whether I fired five shots or six . . . FEEL LUCKY, PUNK?
- You know, I've heard tell that there's a special hell where bad kids go. All they've got there are brussels sprouts and year-round school.
- Go ahead. Make my day.
- I'm going to move to Connecticut, now. Where are you going?
- I guess I should tell you the truth. I didn't really buy the stun gun for burglars.
- You're going to sleep over at your Aunt Betty's tonight while your mother and I build a moat.
- You know, if I attacked a kid like you with the weed trimmer, there isn't a court in the land that would convict me.
- Shape up right now! Or I'll tell you about the way life was when I was a kid.
- How would you like to go to school in last year's styles?

- As soon as they invent a time machine, I'm going to go back to 1964 and have myself sterilized.
- See the moose head over the fireplace? That could be you.
- One more comment out of you and I'll send the barber secret instructions to give you a dorky haircut.
- I'm just going to get the phone book and see if the Pied Piper of Hamlin has a listing.
- Surprise! The Marine Corps just lowered the enlistment age to seven.
- Clean up your room or I'm going to begin lobbying for the repeal of child labor laws.
- I'm afraid your behavior merits a straight week of eggplant and stewed beets.
- According to a clause in your adoption papers, we can give you back at any time.
- Did I fail to mention that there's not enough room in the bomb shelter for you?
- You can either eat your green beans or I'll tell you what they really put in hot dogs.
- Believe me! . . . The Elephant Man was just a guy who ate too much greasy food as a teenager. . . . You can look it up.
- If you ever do that again, I'll die on the spot and rack you with untold guilt for the rest of your life.
- Next time you do that, I'm going to explain in detail an average day inside a state prison.
- Doctors now believe that smarting off to your father can lead to blindness and insanity.
- If you ever want to see your Cabbage Patch doll in one piece again, clean your room.
- You know, when you kids make that much noise, Daddy can't even hear the voices inside his head telling him to jump off the garage.

- That's right—honest—I know magic words that will make all the music videos in the whole world disappear.
- Was that your bicycle in the driveway out there? Gee, wish I'd known that before I mashed it into scrap with the station wagon.
- It's just that kind of behavior that causes Mister Rogers to say those horrible things about you.
- You know, I've heard of entire chain gangs made up of kids who won't eat vegetables.
- Sure, I'll be happy to forward your comic books to San Quentin.
- If I may speak bluntly . . . if you don't get at least a C in algebra, you'll spend the rest of your life selling newspapers and drooling profusely.
- Don't want to go to camp, huh? How 'bout something in a Trappist monastery?
- Premarital sex? No, I can't say I ever knew anyone who tried it and lived. Most of them die from hideous diseases, you know.
- Just a word about drugs. There aren't enough in the whole world to deaden the pain you'll receive at the hands of your mother and me.
- I hear the French Foreign Legion is looking for summer help.
- Let me run through the social calendar in a convent just one more time.
- Here's a copy of *Oliver Twist*, a non-fiction account of kids who failed to heed their parents' pleas to get into a good college.

20

Fathers and Prisoners of War: Twenty-five Similarities

After times of war, stories about the treatment of those taken prisoner always surface. Who has not heard these morbid tales of wartime incarceration? It is a testament to the human spirit that some can endure weeks, months, even years of what constitutes the bleakest circumstances, where poor food, inhuman health conditions and atrocious punishments are daily fare. It is no wonder that America often accords its most esteemed honors to those who have experienced the physical and spiritual desolation of the prison camp.

However, society often blissfully ignores another of its heroes, one who also knows the face of deprivation. For the father, who must suffer the demoralizing effects of meager nutrition (In times of desperation, some fathers have been known to eat ham loaf) and substandard accommodations in which plastic slipcovers are not unusual, the world is a stalag of loneliness, despair and unmatched socks. He may live in a suburb and shuttle to work in a carpool, but he is a prisoner, nonetheless—a captive of his credit cards, a plaything for those who would plunder his paycheck and bludgeon his dreams. There is no one to honor his memory with a wreath or speech, no military pension, no twenty-year reunion. His uniform may only be a threadbare cardigan and his post a split-level with a balloon mortgage, but he too is a hero.

Both the prisoner of war and the father have:
1. Cheap haircuts
2. Other guys they know who are in the same bind
3. Rickets
4. Work detail
5. A taste for gruel
6. A tunnel in progress
7. A fear of Spam
8. Known electric shock (For fathers, this accompanies the opening of the utility bill.)
9. Diminished sexual drive
10. Low self-esteem (For fathers this occurs around the second mortgage.)
11. Ill-fitting clothes
12. Flashbacks
13. Sadistic captors
14. A sickly pallor (Explained by vitamin deficiencies and occasional beatings.)
15. Either a strong faith or none at all—depending upon how each views God's responsibility in all of this
16. A hunger for news from the "outside"
17. An occasional bout of head lice
18. A buddy who didn't make it
19. Last year's shoes
20. A desire for vengeance

21. Cigarettes that are used to buy favors and small luxuries
22. A hidden bottle of cheap hooch
23. A rich fantasy life
24. An old picture of Betty Grable
25. A mattress and a bowl (However, the father is buying his on time.)

21

Teenagers: The Early Warning Signs

Maybe it was during a 2 A.M. feeding. Or perhaps the thought arose while watching the child take his first steps. Sooner or later, though, every father makes the realization that the rosy cheeked, gurgling infant nestled in his arms is doomed to become a . . . TEENAGER.

It's difficult at first for the father to come to grips with such a horrifying fact. Naturally, his first concerns are for his child. The usual questions haunt him. Will there be a cure for acne? Will my child have friends and will I allow them in the house? What were the names of those venereal diseases again?

Soon, however, the father begins to contemplate his own well being. More questions. Will my kid be able to beat me up? Will he shun my values and lifestyle by joining a cult that doesn't believe in contemporary hairstyles? Will my son wear a black leather jacket on holidays? Will my daughter acquire a reputation known to sailors in foreign lands? Will my kids stick me in a rest home and only come to visit me on even-numbered birthdays?

Where teenagers are concerned, the fears of the well-worn father are many.

When the father awakens to the notion that twelve or thirteen years down the road his child will go through a transformation that makes Lon Chaney's werewolf problem seem like a mild case of the vapors, he begins to conjure up futile methods of staving off the teenage years.

"Betty, get me the adhesive tape. I'm gonna bind little Tommy. If we hurry, we can still keep him from growing into a (sob, sniff) . . . TEEN-AGER."

Some fathers cope with the inevitable in other ways. State institutions are filled with children who were never picked up from summer camp. And yet other fathers wait to take action until the very last minute, when they give the child a potentially hazardous thirteenth birthday present.

"Now, Billy, I know you had your heart set on the minibike, but I went ahead and got you the Harley-Davidson anyway. Sure, go ahead . . . take her for a spin. I cleared it with Mom."

Sometimes an ocean cruise is given:

"Honey, don't think of it as losing your daughter at sea. Think of it as not having the family name tarnished by teenage pregnancy."

The sooner the father realizes that raising teenagers is a natural part of fatherhood, the sooner he'll be able to plan positive (and legal) strategies for dealing with his little hormonal monsters. Therefore, every father should be aware of the warning signs that signal the onset of (sob, sniff) THE TEENAGE YEARS.

WARNING SIGNS

1. Your child begins to eat great quantities of anything that cannot escape under its own power.
2. The little chap who once crawled up into your lap is now sporting a mustache.
3. You keep finding your daughter's name in phone booths.
4. Your child begins to refer to you as "Pops."
5. A third car suddenly appears in your driveway.
6. Your child resumes sleeping eighteen to twenty hours a day.
7. You catch your child hiding controlled substances in a hollow compartment inside his old teddy bear.
8. Your child yells at you more than you yell at your child.
9. The child who once seemed glued to you now refuses to be seen with you in public.
10. You no longer think the rest home sounds so bad.

22

Fatherly Respect

Vacation by interstate. Cruel and unusual punishment, where fatherly skills are pushed to their limits. It is 1962. My younger brother and I are sitting in the back seat of the family Rambler, light years from our suburban sanctuary, between home and Yellowstone. The ride has been long and hot, yet there's still no sign of Cactus Pete's, WORLD'S LARGEST REPTILE RANCH AND BUTTERSCOTCH FUDGE EMPORIUM UNDER ONE ROOF, whose coming has been heralded by billboards for the last 135 miles.

I have exhausted five Superman comics and two *Mad* magazines, top-of-the-line, back seat reading material. My brother is rummaging through his own stack of pulp heroes when the temptation becomes too great.

I teasingly poke an index finger into his ribs and flick the hair on the back of his head. He screams. He always screams.

As certain as the fly-by of Halley's Comet, our father, who at the helm of the station wagon is guiding us toward a week in a rented cabin, sweeps the back seat with a powerful, beefy palm. Like a martial artist, he is confident and completely in control. THWAAAAAAAAAAAAAAK! woooooooooooSSSSH, THWAK-THWAK! Without his eyes once wandering from the road, he has managed to slap two lapfuls of comics onto the floor and cuff our knees (protruding from plaid Bermudas) on the return swing. He has quelled another uprising. And we are good for at least another twelve miles.

To this day I'm a little apprehensive whenever I'm forced into a back seat. There's a little nervous tic that takes hold of me as I imagine a sweeping right hand clearing the back seat with the vigor of Godzilla taking out downtown Tokyo. But times are changing.

The other day I was passing through the frozen foods aisle of a supermarket when what looked like a fairly typical nuclear family came shuffling from the other direction. The father was burly and looked accustomed to outside labor. His wife was thin and attractive, dressed in a halter and shorts. But riding the front of a shopping cart was their impish-looking son, impish in the same way that Charles Manson is impish. The kid had a frozen ice with a thin straw sticking up from the top. Then, like a Ninja assassin sensing just the right time to strike, the kid blew a fragment of ice at his old man, hitting him smack-dab in the eyeball.

Suddenly the barrel-chested father with the bricklayer arms doubled over and pawed frantically at his right eye. His wife, who seemed used to such antics, whined, "Whaaat now, fer Christ-sake?"

"Him again!" screamed the father pointing at his snickering son, who now clutched the shopping cart with one hand and waved his frozen ice in victory. "He blew some more of that crap in my eye."

I could watch no more. One of my own was drowning in the quicksand of fatherhood, and there wasn't thing-one I could do about it. Oh, I suppose I could have sneaked up behind this shopping cart-riding devil and cracked his skull with a frozen box of cauliflower, but that wouldn't have liberated my poor counterpart. No, freedom was something he had to want, and this incident showed me that he was long used to such abuse.

As the little family shuffled off in the direction of produce, I had to wonder. Could it be that this sandlot gremlin kept his father around for sport, rushing him periodically with some new food product turned weapon? I also speculated about the new tortures the child-monster would devise in the fruits and vegetables. A fast-ball avocado to the groin? A large honeydew to the temple? Or perhaps a slow and painful death by eggplant?

I wondered, too, if Donahue would take note of this trend, the waiving by our younger generation of any small respect for fathers, and some day devote an hour to fathers battered and abused.

> "Today victimized fathers of the very young will recount what it's like to live in terror as a breadwinner."

Could it be that at this very moment, in some church basement, a bunch of fathers was banding together as a support group, swapping ghoulish tales of fatherly disrespect?

"Well . . . I guess I might as well tell you . . . uh
. . . OK . . . Last week, see, I accidentally stepped
on little Ernie's Mr. Potato Head . . . just by acci-
dent, I swear, you gotta believe me. Well, he was
livid, really crazy. He caught me while I was
sleeping and started pounding those little plastic facial parts into my head. . . . Oh, God! . . . It
was a nightmare. . . ."

I couldn't help but speculate on how my own father, he of
the sweeping right and icy stare, might have handled the
supermarket atrocity:

Our family is shuffling through the frozen foods aisle.
(Families have always shuffled in supermarkets, according to most sources, and probably always will.) I blow ice
through a straw and hit my father's eye. I run like a thief.
My father leaps the mixed vegetables with the grace and
power of a jungle cat, and he collars me by the TV dinners.
He dangles me in his hand like a marionette, and he moves
in for the kill. With his other hand, he straddles my skull,
like a crane about to hoist a steel girder.

"Listen, mister, what are you trying to do, blind me?
Answer me, RIGHT NOW!"

The question makes the hairs on the back of my neck
stand up. (If this were not a hypothetical situation, there
would today be a nervous tic that would come over me
whenever I was formally addressed in the frozen foods
aisle of a supermarket.)

"Keep it up, mister. Just keep it up . . . and you'll see
what'll happen."

My heart fills with terror. I break out in a sweat. What
came after a strong head squeeze? Would it pop like a ripe
cantaloupe? Were there punitive techniques that only

fathers knew, like those German generals in late-night movies who always reaffirmed, "Veee haf vays of making you talk, Captain."

I never found out, but I believe. Oh yes, I believe. And *that* is respect.

Modern fatherhood is a lot of things. It is knowing that you'll never again enjoy uninterrupted sleep. It is melted suckers on bucket seats and years of carry-out dinners. It is compromise—giving up carpet for linoleum and trading in the Subaru for a midsize wagon. It is a future without disposable income. It is a day-to-day test of strength and endurance, a trial of man's will, a challenge to his soul.

Beware those who would cloak the whole nasty business in the language of warm and cuddly. Stand your ground and proclaim for all—"FATHERHOOD IS NOT PRETTY."

Gary D. Christenson is a writer and educator whose work has appeared in *TV Guide*. Now thoroughly domesticated, he lives in Elgin, Illinois, with his wife, Debbie, and his sons, Ben and Nate. He has resigned himself to a life of plastic slipcovers, linoleum tile and cars with four doors.